MACMILLAN MODERN DRAMATISTS

Macmillan Modern Dramatists

Series Editors: *Bruce King* and *Adele King*

Published titles

Eugene Benson, *J. M. Synge*

Normand Berlin, *Eugene O'Neill*

Denis Calandra, *New German Dramatists*

Neil Carson, *Arthur Miller*

Ruby Cohn, *New American Dramatists, 1960–1980*

Bernard F. Dukore, *Harold Pinter*

Arthur Ganz, *George Bernard Shaw*

Frances Gray, *John Arden*

Julian Hilton, *Georg Büchner*

Charles R. Lyons, *Samuel Beckett*

Susan Bassnett-McGuire, *Luigi Pirandello*

Leonard C. Pronko, *Eugène Labiche and Georges Feydeau*

Theodore Shank, *American Alternative Theatre*

Nick Worrall, *Nikolai Gogol and Ivan Turgenev*

Further titles are in preparation

MACMILLAN MODERN DRAMATISTS

GEORGE BERNARD SHAW

Arthur Ganz

Professor of English, The City
University of New York

First published 1983 by
THE MACMILLAN PRESS LTD
London and Basingstoke
Companies and representatives throughout the world

Typeset by Wessex Typesetters Ltd
Frome, Somerset

Printed in Hong Kong

ISBN 0 333 28918 8 (hc)
ISBN 0 333 28919 6 (pbk)

Contents

List of Plates		vi
Acknowledgments		vii
Editor's Preface		ix
Introduction		1
1	The Life	5
2	The Life of the Intellect: Political Economy and Religion	27
3	The Life of the Theatre: Shakespeare, Wagner, Ibsen and the Theatre of the Age	54
4	Plays of the Nineties:	77
	Plays Unpleasant	80
	Plays Pleasant	99
	Three Plays for Puritans	119
5	Plays of Maturity:	134
	The Initial Group	134
	Disquisitory Plays on Family and Religion	173
	The Later Group	176
6	Last Plays: *The Apple Cart* and After	202
	Notes	213
	Bibliography	220
	Index	223

List of Plates

1. *You Never Can Tell*, Royal Court Theatre, 1906
2. *Major Barbara*, Royal Court Theatre, 1905
3. *Caesar and Cleopatra*, Savoy Theatre, 1907
4. *Candida*, New York, 1942. Photograph: New York Public Library
5. *The Doctor's Dilemma*, Royal Court Theatre, 1906
6. *Saint Joan*, New Theatre, 1924
7. *Man and Superman*, New York, 1947. Photograph: Eileen Darby
8. *Pygmalion*, His Majesty's Theatre, 1914
9. *Pygmalion*, New York, 1945. Photograph: New York Public Library
10. *The Apple Cart*, Malvern Festival, 1929

Plates 1, 2, 3, 5, 6, 8 and 10 are reproduced by courtesy of the Raymond Mander and Joe Mitchenson Theatre Collection.

Acknowledgments

This book will always be associated in my mind with the Cambridge and New York University libraries, where many of its pages were written. Each has been, in its particular way, a refuge from the demands of academia and, I like to think, a beneficient influence on this work. I have been most fortunate in my Shavian relationships, having been the student of Eric Bentley and Maurice Valency. At my university I have had as friends and colleagues such eminent Shavians as the late Julian Kaye as well as Roger Boxill, Daniel Leary (to whose bibliographical wisdom I am indebted), and Barbara Watson. In addition, I should probably echo the author who is the subject of this book and who once remarked that he would gladly acknowledge those whom he had pillaged if only he could remember them all. Finally, and most importantly, it was the work of my wife, Professor Margaret Ganz, on Shaw, that first set me thinking along the lines followed in this book. I am grateful for that inspiration as well as for an inordinate amount of consideration, and indeed, charity.

Editors' Preface

The *Macmillan Modern Dramatists* is an international series of introductions to major and significant nineteenth- and twentieth-century dramatists, movements and new forms of drama in Europe, Great Britain, America and new nations such as Nigeria and Trinidad. Besides new studies of great and influential dramatists of the past, the series includes volumes on contemporary authors, recent trends in the theatre and on many dramatists, such as writers of farce, who have created theatre 'classics' while being neglected by literary criticism. The volumes in the series devoted to individual dramatists include a biography, a survey of the plays, and detailed analysis of the most significant plays, along with discussion, where relevant, of the political, social, historical and theatrical context. The authors of the volumes, who are involved with theatre as playwrights, directors, actors, teachers and critics, are concerned with the plays as theatre and discuss such matters as performance, character interpretation and staging, along with themes and contexts.

BRUCE KING
ADELE KING

For
RICHARD GANZ

Introduction

'To younger men', Shaw wrote of his opinions, 'they are already outmoded'. This sentence is the more remarkable for occurring in the letter to A. B. Walkley that Shaw used as Preface to *Man and Superman*, the grand dramatic exposition in which he first made explicit his religious ideas. That Shaw could recognise the transience of his 'forms of thought' even as he presented them suggests that what seems his dogmatism is often no more than a comic stance, further tempered by his sense that he too was a phase in evolutionary development. His opinions, he continues, 'will grow shabbier until they cease to count at all', and then, he adds, 'my books will either perish, or, if the world is still poor enough to want them, will have to stand . . . by quite amorphous qualities of temper and energy'. But these qualities are sufficiently amorphous for Shaw himself to have trouble distinguishing them. Insisting that only didacticism can produce a true style ('"for art's sake" alone I would not face the toil of writing a single sentence'), he grants that nevertheless 'all the

1

assertions get disproved sooner or later' and that what remains is 'a magnificent débris of artistic fossils, with the matter-of-fact credibility gone clean out of them, but the form still splendid'.

To live by 'qualities of temper and energy' is one thing; to write in the hope that one's work might some day become an artistic fossil is quite another. In this matter Shaw is a child of his age, which is to say a contemporary of Pater and Wilde, seeing art in the terms set forth by the aesthetes. But it would be hard to argue now that Shaw's plays owe their permanence to the splendour of their 'form'. They have, of course, an assured place in dramatic history, but it is a place not always easy to locate. The influence of his great contemporaries – Ibsen, Strindberg, Chekhov – on subsequent drama is visible enough, but Shaw's remains obscure. Nor can Shaw himself provide more than a hint, although in his characteristic pedagogical style he seems to explain all. 'When I began', he wrote towards the end of his life, 'the London stage was crowded with French dramatizations of police and divorce cases spoilt by the translators in deference to British prudery. . . . Speeches of more than twenty words were considered impossible and too long: I knocked all that into a cocked hat by giving my characters religions, politics, professions and human nature'. But the Shavian style, though it may have suggested rhetorical possibilities, remains inimitable; the religious and political questions that Shaw argues so vividly in the Prefaces tend to be less crucial in the plays themselves; the profession he dealt with most explicitly was the oldest, Mrs Warren's, but the thesis he advances with regard to it is not the hinge on which his play turns, nor are other plays that deal with 'professional' concerns (e.g. *Major Barbara, The Doctor's Dilemma*) centred on them. Without denying Shaw's assertion that he had opened the drama to wider interests, one is finally left with the claim which seems most conventional and may in fact be most radical: that his contribution had been to give his characters 'human nature'.

It seems at first a curious claim to be advanced by, or on behalf of, a playwright who has been accused of making his personages mere mouthpieces for his own views. Nor is the accusation invariably unjust: when Nicola of *Arms and the Man* cautions the impetuous Louk against offending their employers ('you dont know the power such high people have over the like of you and me when we try to rise out of our poverty against them'), we hear the voice not of a Bulgarian servant but of an English socialist. Such occasions, however, are rare. The voice of Vivie Warren is not that of Candida Morell, nor the voice of Jack Tanner that of Henry Higgins. Nevertheless, though these voices keep their individual timbres and speak to us of very different matters – of self-assertion, of maternal power, of sexual force, of linguistic creation – they all sound a common note. All of these figures, and indeed all of the crucial Shavian characters, whatever their genuine concerns with religion, politics, and professions, are deeply involved with those central familial relationships, including sexual relations, that more than any others define our 'human nature'. That many of these are symbolic does not make them any less real: Caesar's connection with Cleopatra, for example, is quite as paternal as Undershaft's with Barbara, having to do in both cases with questions of education, parental authority, and filial selfhood. That many of them involve negation makes them no less significant: Higgins' refusal of Eliza's demands is at least as meaningful as Tanner's yielding to Ann Whitefield's blandishments.

If a certain severity informs these Shavian relationships,

it is that Shaw's own temper and upbringing offered him glimpses of our human circumstances denied to less penetrating and more equable natures. What Shaw chose to look at he saw, in the special light of his comic vision, with extraordinary, at times disturbing clarity. Strangely, the very exuberance of that comic energy (to return to those 'amorphous qualities of temper and energy' of which Shaw spoke) tends to mask the austerity of the Shavian vision. So endearing are Shaw's comic creations that one sometimes fails to recognise how complex, even disquieting is their emotive environment. So positive is Shaw's vision of social and evolutionary progress that one hardly notices how disabused is his view of the human present and how profound his desire to transcend it. From the tension of these contradictory elements arises the Shavian drama, at once lucid and optimistic, elusive and despairing. It is the most notable body of drama to be written in English, perhaps in any language, since Shakespeare. It is a large body of work, and Shaw has been accused of being garrulous. The words he composed for the god Ra in the Prologue to *Ceasar and Cleopatra* – evoking two of his heroes, Bunyan and Goethe – are his best defence:

'I had not spoken so much but that it is in the nature of a god to struggle for ever with the dust and the darkness, and to drag from them, by the force of his longing for the devine, more life and more light'.

4

1
The Life

In 1934 a letter was dropped into a post box in England; the address on the envelope consisted of the word 'To', followed by a sketchy caricature of Shaw, and printed underneath it 'LONDON or-where-ever-he-happens-to-be-at-the-moment!' It reached its destination.

These circumstances testify in part to Shaw's eminence as the most notable English-speaking playwright since Shakespeare, but also to his status as a public figure, to the force with which he had imposed the glittering persona of G. B. S. – artist, prophet, and clown – not only upon the British postal service but upon his age. That he did so despite adverse early circumstances is more than a tribute to his genius; for him this achievement must have amounted to an act of faith. In the private religion of Creative Evolution that Shaw came to profess, a creature can be raised through the action of the Life Force within him to a higher state of being. For the awkward, half-educated Irish youth who came to London in 1876, to have transformed himself into G. B. S. by sheer effort of will

5

was hardly a less momentous act. When he wrote a play about a flower girl who in acquiring a new speech acquires a new soul, Shaw was dramatising a central action of his life. Indeed, it was an action he carried beyond his life. That Shaw chose to leave a large part of his considerable fortune to a project for the reform of the alphabet seemed to many the decision of an elderly crank. But it marked for Shaw an effort to take the very language itself, the instrument with which he had made his life, his self, and his art, and to raise it to a higher state of being.

But such considerations were far in the future on 26 July 1856, when Lucinda Elizabeth Gurly, the wife of George Carr Shaw, gave birth to their third and last child, their only son, at their house on Upper Synge Street (33 Synge Street in its present numbering) in Dublin. He was christened George Bernard, though in later life he made little use of the name he shared with his father. Having been born into the Ascendancy, the Protestant class whose ancestors were mostly British settlers in Ireland, Shaw might have expected prosperity and a genteel upbringing. In comparison to a child of Catholic agricultural labourers, who made up the majority of the population of a poor and at times famine-stricken country, he had advantages, but they were of a very limited kind. Shaw's mother was the daughter of an impecunious and unscrupulous country landowner 'whose rule was', as Shaw said, 'when in difficulties, mortgage'.[1] Anxious to escape the tyrannical strictness of the aunt who had brought her up after the death of her mother and on bad terms with her father who was about to remarry, she accepted the proposal of a man seventeen years her senior and did so despite the angry warnings of her relations that he drank. On the wedding trip she was distressed to discover that his protestations of abstinence, which he

6

evidently contrived to believe himself, were false; by then it was too late.

The household into which Shaw was born four years later was not a financially comfortable one. Through family influence Shaw's father had procured a sinecure in the Dublin Law Courts; though his post was abolished, he received a pension, which he sold, investing the proceeds in a corn milling firm. He was not a competent businessman, but the firm, running largely, in Shaw's words, 'by its own momentum', lasted out his lifetime, providing a modest, if sometimes precarious living. In the social code of the age a wholesale business, however marginal its profits, was a dignified occupation suitable to the second cousin of a baronet – as the elder Shaw was – whereas a retail establishment, however handsomely it paid, would have been an unthinkable breach of decorum. Shaw's amused vision of such dubious distinctions appears in Act III of *Major Barbara* when Stephen, insisting that he does not want to enter the cannon business because it would mean going 'into trade', goads his mother into announcing grandly, 'Cannons are not trade, Stephen. They are enterprise'.[2] Although Shaw could laugh at such delusions, he never deceived himself about the need for money, having known for too long the frustrations of his class, those who had claims to gentility but, unlike the self-made upstarts, lacked the means to realise them. 'I was a downstart', he wrote, 'and the son of a downstart'.

'I can only imagine the hell into which my mother descended', he suggested elsewhere, 'when she found out what shabby-genteel poverty with a drunken husband is like'. Shaw himself discovered his father's weakness when the two were out for a walk and the elder Shaw, playing with his son, almost threw him into a canal. Returning home, the shocked child confided to his mother, 'Mamma:

I think Pappa is drunk', only to have her reply, 'When is he anything else?' It is easy enough to recognise that Shaw owed much of his lifelong abstinence from alcohol to his revulsion from his father's habit, but Erik Erikson suggests, more subtly, a transformation of the parental compulsion into part of the 'inner defenses' of the youthful Shaw. Quoting a passage from Shaw's autobiographical writings, Erikson points out (italicising key phrases) how 'the great wit almost coyly admits his psychological insight: "I have risen by sheer gravitation, too industrious by acquired habit to stop working (*I work as my father drank*)" '.[3] But that Shaw could not always convert his father's compulsions to his own advantage is implied as Erikson finds 'a more unconscious level of Shaw's oedipal tragedy . . . in what looks like a screen memory of his father's impotence: Shaw recalls his father when drunk "with an *imperfectly wrapped up goose under one arm* and *a ham in the same condition under the other . . . butting* at the garden wall in the belief that he was *pushing open the gate*, and *transforming his tall hat into a concertina* in the process"'. Remarking that 'the psychosexual elements in Shaw's identity could find a solid anchor point in this memory,' Erikson leads one to speculate that the late beginning and early termination of Shaw's active sexual life might suggest an identification with his father's deficiencies. A happier paternal influence was claimed by Shaw himself, who maintained that he inherited 'and used with much effect' his father's 'humorous sense of anticlimax', citing the elder Shaw's rebuke to his son for scoffing at the Bible, followed by the earnest assurance that 'even the worst enemy of religion could say no more of the Bible than that it was the damndest parcel of lies ever writen'.

As this passage indicates, Shaw received the minimum of

conventional religious training; nor indeed, was there much social training. Disappointed in her marriage, uninterested in and ignorant of domestic matters, their mother turned over the running of her household and the raising of the boy and his two sisters to illiterate and ill-paid servants. (Shaw said that his horror of the slum tenements into which his nursemaid took him when she was supposed to be giving him exercise in the parks ultimately resulted in the denunciation of poverty as a crime in *Major Barbara*.) Just as problematic as her neglect of her children was Mrs Shaw's remote, strangely equable nature. 'She was neither weak nor submissive; but as she never revenged,' Shaw wrote of her, 'so also she never forgave. There were no quarrels and consequently no reconciliations.' At the moment when Shaw seems most to admire her he is also at his most implacable: 'Under all the circumstances it says a great deal for my mother's humanity that she did not hate her children. She did not hate anybody, nor love anybody'. One is reminded of the moment in *Caesar and Cleopatra* when another remote yet beneficent figure is described by his surrogate child in almost the same words: 'Caesar loves no one,' Cleopatra says and, noting that ordinary people are dominated by hatred of those they do not love, adds, 'But it is not so with Caesar. He has no hatred in him'. That so many of the Shavian saints have lofty but impersonal parental natures – Higgins, Undershaft, Shotover come immediately to mind – suggests that in his art Shaw was transforming into an exalted if ambiguous virtue what must have been in his life the source of a central emotional deprivation.[4]

But if Mrs Shaw could not give her son care and affection, she did offer him access to what irradiated his life and his art – music. Possessed, according to Shaw, of 'a mezzo-soprano voice of remarkable purity of tone,' she was instructed by a neighbouring music teacher, George John Vandeleur Lee, a bachelor living with his brother, who trained her voice so well that it lasted unimpaired till her death in her eighties. She quickly became not only the prima donna in the many musical events Lee directed, but chorus leader and Lee's 'general musical factotum'. Soon rehearsals were held in the Shaw drawing-room, and after the death of Lee's brother, the households were merged. In 1866, when Shaw was ten, Lee and the Shaw family moved to Torca Cottage, a house on a hill above Dublin Bay, and then alternated between it and 1 Hatch Street, a suitably fashionable establishment for Lee's lessons and more substantial than the Shaws could afford unaided. Some biographers have suspected sexual relations between Mrs Shaw and Lee, but Shaw himself dismissed the idea, insisting that the connection should not be 'unpleasantly misunderstood'.[5] In any case, the result of Lee's presence in the household (aside from the fact that his personal magnetism tended to efface the elder Shaw) was that as a boy Shaw had the greatest vocal music of the preceding century constantly in his ears. Eventually Shaw taught himself the piano well enough to play reductions of orchestral scores and to be a reasonably proficient accompanist. Not only did this background help him become the most brilliant music reviewer of his day but it ultimately contributed to the uniquely musical balancing of voices in his dramatic dialogue.

Shaw always insisted that his exposure to music, to the other arts (derived partly from hours spent wandering in the Dublin National Gallery), and to nature was far more significant than his classroom education. This disclaimer from the Preface to *London Music* is typical:

At the end of my schooling I knew nothing of what the

school professed to teach; but I was a highly educated boy all the same. I could sing and whistle from end to end leading works by Handel, Haydn, Mozart, Beethoven, Rossini, Bellini, Donizetti, and Verdi. I was saturated with English literature from Shakespear and Bunyan to Byron and Dickens. And I was so susceptible to natural beauty that, having had some glimpse of the Dalkey scenery on an excursion, I still remember the moment when my mother told me that we were going to live there as the happiest of my life.

Of the various private schools that Shaw attended only one is significant, but not for educational reasons. In February of 1869 Shaw was sent, at Lee's suggestion, to the Central Model Boys' School, an institution that catered for the children of lower-middle-class Catholics. To a child of the Ascendancy, the loss of social status was horrifying. Not only did the boy refuse to return in September, but the grown writer did not reveal the incident till late in life, having concealed it from his biographers, even from his wife. This 'snob tragedy', as Shaw himself called it, suggests more than the way in which a social attitude may persist even in one who no longer consciously accepts it (Shaw found his family's claims to exalted gentility at once amusing and contemptible); it hints at something central to his work. That Shaw was a socialist might lead one to suppose incautiously that he was a democrat, but such is not the case. When, for example, Undershaft says that he and Cusins and Barbara 'must stand together above the common people' to help their children climb up to a higher level, he evokes the Shavian admiration for a spiritual aristocracy that far transcends, and yet is rooted in, the supposed social aristocracy whose values Shaw denigrated but whose influence he did not quite escape.

11

When Shaw was fifteen, the formal education that he later professed to despise – though he did well in his last school – ended. Through the influence of a relative, he was taken on as a junior clerk at the prestigious Townshend estate agents. Again he did well; within a year he was head cashier, his salary having quintupled. When around this time Lee, ambitious for wider success, left Ireland to set up as a music teacher in London, the problem of how the household could continue without his resources was solved by Mrs Shaw's decision to break up her family and go to London. She planned to become a music teacher in her own right and to further the singing career of her elder daughter, Lucy. Thus the circumstances of Shaw's family changed significantly. Although Shaw's father assisted in this arrangement by generously making his family an allowance of one pound a week for the rest of his life, Shaw may have exaggerated his father's relief at being, in effect, deserted by his wife and daughters, 'they took off his shoulders a burden he was unable to bear and glad to discard', the son claimed. Shaw remained with the estate agents till 1876 (the year his younger sister died of tuberculosis), when, to his employer's understandable distress, he resigned. Putting behind him, as he said, '(a few private friendships apart) no society that did not disgust me', Shaw left Dublin – not to return for almost thirty years – to join his mother in London.

He arrived at her house in Victoria (now Netherton) Grove off Fulham Road in the full splendour of a four-wheeled carriage, too awkward and shy to risk the smaller hansom, having realised in a moment of panic at Euston Station that he did not know how to manage its door. (Marchbanks' difficulties with the cabman in *Candida* may owe something to Shaw's memories of the occasion.) He was received with neither ill-will nor enthusiasm; after a

12

brief visit to the grave of his younger sister, Agnes, on the Isle of Wight, he settled down to remain in his mother's household until his marriage at forty-three. For nine years, till he began to make his way as a reviewer, Shaw had almost no income. Later in life he delighted in presenting a diabolonian picture of himself as a ruthless young artist who had stooped to living off the labours of an aging parent ('I threw my mother into the struggle for life'), but in doing so he was boasting of a relationship that, as he also admitted, in actuality barely existed ('My mother and I lived together but there was hardly a word between us'). Indeed, Shaw, who had supported himself since he was fifteen, hardly cost his mother very much: his room was available in any case; the meals carelessly prepared by a servant amounted to little; the clothes he had brought with him ultimately became so shabby that he almost ceased to be presentable.

For three years Shaw's life had no central focus. He crammed for a Civil Service exam, gave it up to ghost write music criticism for Vandeleur Lee, studied French, read Shelley, learned harmony and counterpoint, and wandered about London planning 'extravagant social reforms'. But 1879 was a turning point: in that year Shaw finished one career and began two more. Prodded by his sister Lucy into a final encounter with commercial employment, once more arranged through a family connection, he worked for the Edison Telephone Company of London from November 1879 till June 1880. Although his efficiency again won him promotion as well as an invitation to reapply when the Edison and Bell companies merged and employees were formally dismissed, he did not do so. He had other aims.

Just before Shaw started work for the Edison Company, he had completed his first novel, *Immaturity*, begun the previous March. Although there had been no earlier

13

indications of a serious determination to be a novelist, once he had begun, he applied himself with the same meticulous diligence he had shown in business, each day filling five pages of the exercise books in which he wrote, stopping in the middle of a sentence if that was where the page ended, producing double the amount if he missed a day. At this time, by no coincidence, he seems to have begun another creation, that of the public persona, ultimately called G. B. S.; a photograph of the period shows him with the faint beginnings of the beard behind which he lived for the rest of his life. The mercurial element in that persona masked a fierce tenacity, for despite refusal after refusal from publishers, Shaw continued to produce a novel a year till 1883 when, after two vast chapters of *An Unsocial Socialist*, he finally gave up a medium for which he was not suited. Between 1884 and 1888 the novels were published, largely as filler material, in a socialist journal, *To-Day,* and a 'rationalist' family magazine, *Our Corner.* None of these works is a success as a novel; none fails to suggest something significant about its author and the development of his mind.

Meanwhile, as Shaw worked on the novels, he not only made himself into a fluent writer, he acquired another verbal skill of almost equal significance. At Vandeleur Lee's he met a musical authority named James Lecky (whose parallel interest in phonetics led him to introduce Shaw to the Oxford phonetician Henry Sweet, the model for Henry Higgins of *Pygmalion*). Late in 1880, when Lecky took Shaw to one of the meetings of a debating group, the Zetetical ('seeking') Society, Shaw abruptly spoke – for the first time before an audience. Despite his desperate nervousness, a compulsion to speak in public had seized him, and he resolved to become an accomplished orator 'or perish in the attempt'.

Intriguingly, this resolution preceded Shaw's conversion to socialism, even though he ultimately devoted most of the extraordinary oratorical skill he acquired to propagandising Fabian reforms. Maurice Valency's suggestion that Shaw 'practiced his oratory with the single-minded absorption of an opera singer' is, perhaps unintentionally, illuminating.[6] Drawn to master public speaking by precisely this element of vocal, quasi-operatic performance, the timid, awkward youth could unconsciously emulate, even identify with, the mother who had rejected him for her singing and perhaps hope to displace his sister, the preferred sibling, who, despite her undistinguished operatic career, had allowed herself to accuse him of being idle and lazy. If this strategy was a failure psychologically (Mrs Shaw remained herself to the end), it was a success aesthetically; to the verbal fluency acquired in five years of novel writing Shaw added the balanced oratorical cadences combined with conversational ease uniquely characteristic of his style.

A young clerk in the Colonial Office, Sidney Webb, whom Shaw met at the Zetetical Society, was to become, with his wife, Beatrice, a lifelong companion in the great Fabian project of socialist advocacy. Although Sidney Webb did not always speak well of Shaw, whose exuberance and inability to resist a joke would sometimes offend people, Shaw never deviated in his admiration for Webb, whose capacity for work and ability to absorb information exceeded even his own. But Shaw was not yet a socialist, though he joined numerous intellectual societies and, as he said, 'infested' public meetings, grasping the occasions to speak 'in the streets, in the parks, at demonstrations, anywhere and everywhere possible'. A lecture in September of 1882 by a 'handsome and eloquent' American, Henry George, who argued for a set of economic reforms to counter the poverty created by the development of capitalism, led Shaw to read George's *Progress and Poverty* and be 'swept into the Great Socialist Revival of 1883'. Shortly after the lecture Shaw attended a meeting of a Marxist group, the Social Democratic Federation, founded by Henry Mayers Hyndman. Having spoken in the debate, Shaw was condescendingly informed that one who had not read Marx was not entitled to discuss socialism. There being as yet no English translation of *Das Kapital*, Shaw retired to what was, in effect, his private library, the British Museum, and read it in French. (William Archer, who had not then met Shaw, noticed the red-haired young man studying alternately the translation of Marx and the score of *Tristan und Isolde*.) 'I was a coward,' Shaw said later, 'until Marx made a Communist of me and gave me a faith: Marx made a man of me'.[7]

He did not, however, remain a Marxian revolutionist, though he kept his 'faith' in socialism, as he kept other faiths he acquired in his youth (for example, the Shelleyan vegetarianism he had adopted in 1881, partly in the hope that it would cure his severe monthly headaches, partly because vegetarian restaurants, then opening in London, were cheap). Early in 1884 Shaw read the first tract published by the Fabian Society; he joined it later that year and brought Webb into the group. Although the society's name derived from Hannibal's opponent, the Roman general Quintus Fabius Maximus Cunctator, and referred to the latter's supposed injunction to wait for the opportune moment and then to strike hard, the term 'Fabian' eventually came to suggest the gradualism, concern with specific social reform, and commitment to education and parliamentary action that marked the path followed, in part because of the prodding of the Fabians, by the British Labour Party in its rise to power. Shaw now entered upon the vast unpaid labours that for many years he devoted to the Fabian Society, studying, writing, editing, and – using his now formidable talents as an orator – addressing public meetings, speaking at least three times a fortnight.

At this point in his life Shaw had a mission as a Socialist, a career as a Fabian, and a lively circle of intellectual friends (in whose lives he loved to meddle). 'He is a very clever writer and speaker –' wrote the shrewd wife of a colleague, 'is the grossest flatterer (of men, women, and children impartially) I ever met, is horribly untrustworthy as he repeats everything he hears, and does not always stick to the truth, and is *very plain* . . . and yet is one of the most fascinating men I ever met. Everyone rather affects to despise him "Oh, it's only Shaw." That sort of thing, you know, but everyone admires him all the same'.[8] Nevertheless, still desperately poor, Shaw had no salaried occupation. In 1885 that circumstance was altered by William Archer, journalist, drama critic, and translator of Ibsen, who had now become friends with the remarkable young man from the British Museum and who contrived to get him work as a book reviewer for the *Pall Mall Gazette*. Then Archer, who was drama critic for the weekly journal *The World*, was asked to write the art criticism as well; he agreed but got Shaw to go to the exhibitions with him and tell him what to say. When Shaw refused to accept half of Archer's salary, Archer resigned and got Shaw appointed in his place.

Archer had already done Shaw a far greater service, though neither of them realised it at the time, by proposing that they collaborate on a play. As a student of the drama, Archer felt that he could construct an effective plot, and he believed that his lively friend could write splendid

17

dialogue. Shaw agreed and promptly set to work on a libretto that, in the manner of the day, Archer had fabricated loosely from Émile Augier's *La Ceinture dorée*. Archer's confidence in their success was soon diminished, however, when Shaw explained that he had used up all the plot and, somewhat in the manner of Oliver Twist, asked for more. Archer managed to provide some, but when Shaw called for still more, the collaboration collapsed – though not the friendship – and the manuscript went into Shaw's desk drawer, not to reappear for several years.

Although Shaw's efforts as a dramatist were for the moment abortive, his career as a journalist flourished. For three years he wrote about painting, though art criticism was not his *forte*, but in 1888 he found a true métier. Hired to write leaders for a new paper, *The Star*, he discovered that, though liberal, the paper was not so liberal as to sustain his Fabian editorialising and switched to music criticism, signing his articles Corno di Bassetto. At the time Shaw had never heard a basset horn – though used by his beloved Mozart to accompany an aria in *La Clemenza di Tito* – which had been replaced by the bass clarinet. But he liked the name, if not the sound of the instrument when he finally did hear it. The reviews that Shaw wrote for *The Star* till 1890 and then for *The World* till 1894 (he had resigned as art critic in 1889 but was lured back by a higher salary) raised, by their vivacity and wit, their penetration and charm, the chronicling and judging of musical events to an art in its own right. Even today, when his championing of Wagner and Elgar, his criticism of this or that performance have lost their immediate reason for being, Shaw's confrontations with the musical life of his time still instruct and delight. The same is true for his drama criticism written for *The Saturday Review* from 1895 to 1898, but here a new element is found. To the humour and perceptiveness with which he surveyed the theatrical scene, was added a persistent purpose relevant to his own work. The well-made comedies, the sentimental melodramas, even the productions of Shakespeare with the great actors of the day – grandiose and often brutally cut (of Sir Henry Irving: 'he does not cut plays; he disembowels them') – were impediments to be pushed aside to make room for the new drama awakened by Ibsen and represented in England pre-eminently by Shaw himself. When he published these reviews later, he admitted, with whimsical self-deprecation, that some of his utterances were unjust, were in fact 'not even reasonably fair'. 'I must therefore warn the reader', he continued, 'that what he is about to study is not a series of judgements aiming at impartiality, but a siege laid to the theatre of the XIXth Century by an author who had to cut his own way into it at the point of the pen, and throw some of its defenders into the moat'.[9]

But before Shaw triumphed in his attack on the citadel of literary success, he had one more career – the beginning and ending of which are, only partly by coincidence, precisely those of his career as a journalist – that of, as he called it, a philanderer. Shaw's active sexual life began on his twenty-ninth birthday, 26 July 1885, and may be said to have ended with his unconsummated marriage in 1898.

In April 1885 Shaw's father died; in May, Shaw began to be self-supporting as a book reviewer; in June, he took part of the proceeds of a small insurance policy on his father's life and bought a new suit, finally ridding himself of his shabby appearance; in July, he allowed himself to be seduced ('I was an absolute novice. I did not take the initiative in the matter')[10] by Jenny Patterson, a music pupil of his mother's and a well-to-do widow at least twelve years his senior. This conjunction of circumstances tempts one to suppose that, to put it crudely, the death of Shaw's father allowed him, as it were, to sleep with his mother: which is to say that the removal of the 'impotent' father/rival of Shaw's 'oedipal tragedy' (to use Erikson's language again) enabled him finally to consummate a union with a mother surrogate. But such simplistic Freudianism is always dangerous, particularly here. This conjunction of events, however suggestive, is only part of a complex sequence that surely began with the child Shaw's rejection by an unloving mother who evoked anger and guilt even as she left him free to 'idolize' her (Shaw's term) in supposedly non-sexual fantasy. (Shaw's comments on the relationship between Higgins and his mother in the postscript to *Pygmalion* suggest the limits of his own understanding of such matters.) Whatever the roots of his repressions and despite their force, he was able for a time to lead a sexual life. The affair with Mrs Patterson dragged on for eight years, to Shaw's distress for she was violently jealous and made scenes. The most spectacular of these was a confrontation in the home of another mistress, the actress Florence Farr, during which Shaw had forcibly to restrain Mrs Patterson from attacking her rival. The episode substantially ended their relationship, at the same time providing Shaw with material for *The Philanderer*.

Meanwhile there were numerous flirtations with women in his circle, at one time amounting to six simultaneously. Profoundly attracted to women, desiring to idealise them, aroused but troubled by their sexuality (Shaw never forgot the shock he received as a small boy when fashions in skirts changed and he saw a grown woman's legs for the first time), he remained a compulsive amorist who shied away from intercourse. In his work too, both impulses flower: *Caesar and Cleopatra*, for example, is predicated on a traditionally erotic situation, which Shaw is then at pains to frustrate. Moreover, such plays as *Candida* and *The Devil's Disciple* in which the child/intruder in a household arouses the erotic interest of a wife and then withdraws, paralleled by Shaw's relationships with a number of married couples, confirm the power of his disquieting, even traumatic childhood in shaping his later experience and his art. Shaw's unconsummated marriage (he was on crutches at the ceremony and shortly after contrived to break an arm – the psychologically oriented observer will not find the symbolism obscure) to Charlotte Payne-Townshend, an Irish 'millionairess' somewhat resembling his mother, who confessed that the idea of childbearing was 'physically repugnant' to her, gave him both comfortable domesticity and protection from feminine sexuality, but it did not end what were probably his most satisfactory love affairs, the epistolary ones with two notable actresses of the day.

In the letters he could rhapsodise 'poetically' without the danger of physical demands, in effect playing the beloved child he had not been, and he could lecture them about their art and demand they appear in his works, in effect playing the wise father he had not had. The latter role he dramatised many times: Caesar with Cleopatra, Undershaft with Barbara, Higgins with Eliza are only the most obvious instances. But the maternal element here is no less significant. Daniel Dervin points to a remarkable passage in a letter of June 1897 written to Ellen Terry late one night while Shaw was on a fatiguing train journey. Disturbed by having just seen on an advertisement a picture of her in a low-cut dress, he complains in child-like tones, 'I can't in pen and ink rest these bruised brains in your lap and unburden my heart with inarticulate cries', and then confesses, 'I am particularly tedious at present . . . wanting to sleep, and yet to sleep with you'. In an extraordinary vision he sees her, as a result of their intercourse, flying into the woods the next day and producing hundreds of winged babies who would fly away with her to 'some heavenly country' and then grow into 'strong sweetheart sons' with whom she would 'found a divine race.' 'If you were my mother,' Shaw concludes, 'I am sure I should carry you away . . .'.[11] The powerful incest fantasy here depicted hints at the roots of Shaw's sexual dilemma even as the picture of the flight to the heavenly country and the development of a divine race (of Supermen?) links them to significant elements that will figure later in the plays. The one occasion when Shaw apparently attempted to turn epistolary fantasy into reality – in a seaside assignation with his other notable actress correspondent, Mrs Patrick Campbell – ended in disaster: she departed; he wrote a furious letter. But in the plays private fantasy became art, embodying a vision of sexual relations that, though partial, is none the less at once romantic and cruelly true.

It was in the midst of his efforts as journalist, socialist, and amorist that Shaw at last entered upon his ultimate career as a playwright. Although once he was embarked in the drama, he seems to have recognised it as his true métier, there is no evidence that he had earlier been drawn more profoundly to the theatre than to the other arts. The play he had begun on Archer's libretto had been put aside without much distress. Even his championing of Ibsen's works, with which Archer had acquainted him, was based more on a view of Ibsen as prophet than playwright. And he had expanded a lecture to the Fabian Society into *The Quintessence of Ibsenism* (1891) before he began his work in the theatre. Nevertheless it was, in effect, Ibsen who opened the way for him through the unlikely agency of a Dutch Jewish tea merchant and part-time consular agent who had settled in London. Jacob Thomas Grein's real concern was with *avant-garde* drama; he organised what he called the Independent Theatre, announced a production of *Ghosts*, hired the Royalty Theatre in Soho, and – defying augury – presented the first of two performances on Friday, 13 March 1891. (The economics of the theatre at that time allowed for such sporadic presentations.) Although the play was greeted by what probably remains unchallenged as the most hysterical burst of vituperation in the history of drama criticism ('crapulous stuff . . . absolutely loathsome . . . a dirty act done publicly'), Grein was determined to persevere but could not find a suitable play by an English writer for his next production. Strolling with Shaw late one evening in Hammersmith, he complained of this dearth. When Shaw suggested a work by himself, Grein at once accepted. The two acts of the old Archer play were now resurrected; to them Shaw added a third and entitled the piece *Widowers' Houses*. The Independent Theatre once again presented two performances at the Royalty, the first on 9 December 1892. The furore over *Ghosts* was not repeated. Indeed, the performances were applauded, and there were unusually long reviews and in two papers even editorial articles. Shaw had found his vocation.

Having done so, he entered upon it with characteristic vigour. His next two plays were both written in 1893, though neither was performed for several years, *The Philanderer* because, according to Shaw, it needed a better production than the limited resources of the Independent Theatre could command and *Mrs Warren's Profession* because Grein disliked it and because, with its subject of prostitution and its hint of incest, it was sure to be banned by the Lord Chamberlain. But Shaw was returned to the stage in 1894. Florence Farr had planned a season of noncommercial plays, having been guaranteed financial backing by a well-to-do woman named Annie Elizabeth Horniman, later instrumental in supporting the Abbey Theatre; but when her first production was a disaster, she appealed to Shaw for permission to revive *Widowers' Houses*. Instead, he quickly finished *Arms and the Man*, which had a wildly successful first night (Shaw answered the solitary hiss that interrupted his curtain call with a now legendary riposte: 'I quite agree with you, sir, but what can we two do against so many?') and a substantial run (21 April to 7 July), though it ultimately lost money, costing Miss Horniman (who kept her support secret lest it embarrass her Quaker family) about £2,000. But the play was seen by the actor Richard Mansfield, who took it to America, and Shaw began to have some income as a playwright.

It was at this point in his career (January 1895) that Shaw began his work as a drama critic, appearing at the theatre in his tweed suit and soft hat, a combination of insistent common sense and self-advertisement, when all respectable men wore tall silk hats and frock coats. He went on writing – *Candida, The Man of Destiny, You Never Can Tell* – without theatrical success, indeed with skimpy productions or none. With Shaw's friend, the Ibsen actress Janet Achurch, *Candida* was presented in the provinces by the Independent Theatre and brought to London for two performances. *The Man of Destiny* was rejected by Mansfield, who was Shaw's model for Napoleon, and by Sir Henry Irving, with whom Shaw contrived to quarrel despite, or perhaps in part because of, his epistolary friendship with Irving's co-star, Ellen Terry. *You Never Can Tell* was withdrawn from rehearsal when the Haymarket Theatre Company could do nothing with it, one actress complaining that there were 'no laughs and no exits'. Shaw responded to his disappointments by taking on more work, becoming in 1897 a vestryman of St Pancras and for seven years remaining conscientiously involved in civic administration. In the same year he began to publish his plays, in the process of which he created the rich scene and character descriptions that have since helped to make the reading of plays, especially Shaw's, a literary experience.

Meanwhile, Shaw had been asked by William Terriss, a popular actor of melodramas, to write a play for him. Terriss never appeared in *The Devil's Disciple*, which he had difficulty in following when Shaw read it to him, for by grotesque irony he was stabbed to death at the stage door of the Adelphi, the theatre in which his melodramas were performed. When performed by Mansfield, however, the play was a considerable success in America, the proceeds allowing Shaw to give up reviewing (in May 1898) and to marry without being dependent on his wife's income. But public acceptance in England lay six years in the future. It came finally, through the work of Harley Granville-Barker, a young actor and producer, later a playwright and still later the author of the splendid *Prefaces to Shakespeare*. Barker, whose early performance as Marchbanks in *Candida* Shaw said 'was humanly speaking, perfect', was invited by the manager, J. E. Vedrenne, to direct a Shakespeare revival at the Royal Court, a playhouse outside the regular London theatre circuit and thus cheaper for productions. He agreed, on condition that they also performed six matinées of *Candida*. So successful were these performances, given in the spring of 1904, that in the autumn of that year the Vedrenne-Barker management offered a series of matinées that included performances of Shaw's newest play, *John Bull's Other Island*. The play was revived in the spring and drew fashionable audiences. The Prime Minister, Arthur Balfour, attended four times, bringing distinguished colleagues. Finally, Edward VII 'commanded' a performance and laughed so hard that he broke the elegant chair, rented specially for the occasion, no doubt to the distress of the cautious Vedrenne. But the broken chair was the sign of Shaw's acceptance. He was over fifty by the time the Vedrenne-Barker management at the Royal Court had presented over seven hundred performances of eleven of his works, but he was an established playwright in his adopted country at last.

The remainder of Shaw's career has much of interest, ranging from the settling of his domestic circumstances with the purchase of the house at Ayot St Lawrence that remained his country home till his death at ninety-four, his ambiguous attitude to World War I, his friendships (with T. E. Lawrence, for example), his receipt of the Nobel Prize in 1925, his travels (undertaken in part to please his wife) and his stubborn admiration for dictators. But it is pre-eminently significant for his work in the drama, and that is to be discussed as this book continues.

2
The Life of the Intellect: Political Economy and Religion

If Shaw had not written his plays, few people – perhaps no one – would be much concerned with his labours as a socialist thinker and propagandist or with his convictions as a religious philosopher, although in both areas his achievements, by ordinary standards, would have constituted an honourable life's work. But the standards of history are severe: the career of a distinguished Fabian is by now of interest only to specialists in British political or economic history, that of a latter-day Lamarckian to an even more restricted circle. Nevertheless, Shaw's ideas demand attention from those who would understand his work. Not only do they suggest his relation to the intellectual currents of his age but, in a quite direct way, they appear in his plays. In *Mrs Warren's Profession*, for example, Shaw the socialist slips into the mouth of Crofts, the 'capitalist bully', an unconscious revelation of what

Shaw sees as the pervasive corruption of capitalists society, in which all 'are pocketing what they can' and avoiding 'inconvenient questions.' In a more profound way, Shaw's ideas, transformed into dramatic metaphors, permeate all his plays. The commitment to socialist action in his life becomes in his drama a commitment to human existence in the world, especially as transformed by comedy; at the same time the commitment to the ascendant thrust of the Life Force becomes a darker, to some degree secret, impulse to transcend that world. How this transformation occurs will appear in later discussions of individual plays, but for the present it is important to see just what were Shaw's religious, political, and economic ideas.

The roots of Shaw's socio-economic ideas extend deep into the nineteenth century, at least as far as Carlyle, with his denunciation of the misery engendered by irresponsible economics and his puritanic emphasis on the necessity for work, and as far as Ruskin, with his revulsion from the ugliness of the world created by nineteenth-century capitalism and his distrust of popular democracy. Indeed, Shaw, always endeavouring to present socialism as truly English in ancestry, claims that Ruskin, believing in government by 'an energetic and enlightened minority', was a prophet of 'the Bolshevist party'.[1] Although Shaw said that only Sidney Webb of the early Fabians was directly influenced by John Stuart Mill, nevertheless Mill's advocacy in his later writing of a gradual evolution to socialism through such economic experiments as government acquisition of land for co-operatives and of monopolies, suggests some significant relation to Fabianism.[2]

But neither these figures nor other predecessors provided the systematic, 'scientific' economic basis that Shaw, and indeed the socialist movement, needed. In the

28

early 1880s Shaw seemed to have found what he sought in the work of Marx, the writer who 'made a man' of him, but he did not remain a Marxist for long. Although Shaw never lost his admiration for Marx's optimism, his comprehensive view of history, and especially his 'fine Jewish literary gift, with terrible powers of hatred, invective, irony' that 'exposed the bourgeoisie and made an end of its moral prestige', he soon became convinced that Marx's economics were inadequate.[3] Called upon to defend Marxian ideas by the socialist journal *To-day*, which in 1884 had published an essay critical of Marx by Philip H. Wicksteed, a Unitarian minister and scriptural and literary critic who was interested in economics, Shaw attacked Wicksteed's arguments but ultimately became convinced that his opponent was right. Characteristically, Shaw bore no resentment and became not only Wicksteed's friend but his pupil, studying economics with him in an informal seminar that included distinguished economists and ultimately developed into the Royal Economic Society.

Wicksteed's attack was founded on Marx's commitment to the labour theory of value put forward by the English 'classical' economists (Adam Smith, David Ricardo, etc.), which held essentially that the exchange value of an object was determined by the amount of labour necessary to produce it. Accepting this theory, Marx was able to argue that when the employer takes the 'surplus value', the worth of the labourer's efforts above the wage paid to him, he is expropriating for himself wealth that was created by labour, which is to say that his riches derive from theft.

But this theory upon which so much was founded, in effect the claim to have discerned a moral wrong by intellectual, 'scientific' means, had become vulnerable to attack. In the early 1870s the economist W. Stanley Jevons (and others independently) had postulated an opposing theory of value. The price of manufactured commodities, Jevons argued, is determined not by the amount of labour that went into them but by their utility, by the fact that they are desired. However, since no one will give more money for one unit of the available supply of an article than for another (Jevons' law of indifference) and since additional increments of an article satisfy ever weaker demand for it (his law of the variation of utility), the demand for the final amount of an article that is worth production determines the value of each unit in the total supply.

With the collapse of the labour theory, Marx was, for Shaw, no longer an economist but exclusively a social critic and moralist. Despite his continuing respect for Marx, Shaw had reservations about him even in these roles, for the son of the Anglo-Irish Establishment deeply distrusted Marx's idealisation of the working class, and the puritan activist who had to feel himself the necessary agent of a great purpose, distrusted Marx's insistence on the inevitability of socialism. If socialism was to come, whether by revolution or not, it would need effort and a new economic foundation.

Shaw laid this foundation in a series of articles published in the late 1880s, culminating in 'The Basis of Socialism: Economic', the initial chapter of the *Fabian Essays in Socialism* that Shaw edited for the Fabian Society in 1889. Although Ricardo had led Marx astray with the labour theory, he provided Shaw with the needed alternative in the law of economic rent. Drawing on Ricardo, Shaw illustrates this law by postulating a virgin country in which the first settlers acquire the most productive, best situated land. Later settlers acquire the next most desirable land and so on, until all of the land that is worth farming is under cultivation. If the most profitable land earns £1,000 a year and the least profitable earns £500, then the owner of the best land can rent it for £500 to someone who will farm it and pay him that amount. He can then retire, as a *rentier*, and live without working. In fact, all of the land better than that at the margin of cultivation produces a surplus, which is 'economic rent'. It was this surplus that Shaw's first master in economics, Henry George, had proposed in *Progress and Poverty* to acquire for the general good of the whole community by substituting a single tax on land in place of other sources of government revenue. The socialist solution to the injustice caused by the arbitrary possession of the best land by the first settlers and their heirs was not taxation but acquisition of the land itself by the state, and indeed (profit being a kind of rent) the means of production generally.

In addition, from his study of Jevons, Shaw developed a corollary to support the instituting of socialism. Workers, having no access to land, must sell their labour, that is themselves. But in selling themselves they are selling a commodity subject to the same Jevonian laws as any other. There is, however, a unique factor affecting this commodity: its supply is determined not by market demand but by the irresistible physical impulse to reproduce. Since the supply of labour expands beyond utility and since, by Jevons' law of indifference, all units of the supply are worth the same, the price of labour is even less than the subsistence, as determined by custom, which the classical economists had believed labour could always command. 'This', Shaw wrote, 'is the condition of our English laborers today: they are no longer even dirt cheap: they are valueless and can be had for nothing'.[4] As certain horses would be kept and maintained even if they could be had freely, so some workers would be maintained minimally if their services were desired. Only socialism, Shaw argued, would create genuine wealth and distribute it equitably (*Major Barbara* shows his view of the failure of private redistribution) instead of allowing society to waste itself in producing, beyond certain workers' elementary subsistence, luxuries for the rich, satisfying not real needs but 'the cravings of lust, folly, vanity, gluttony, and madness, technically described by genteel economists as "effective demand"'.[5]

But neither the fierce moral energy behind this contempt for self-indulgence nor Shaw's control of contemporary economic theory could by themselves bring a socialist society into being. To do so an organisation was needed, and Shaw found the one he sought in the Fabian Society. Founded in 1884, it was an off-shoot of the Fellowship of the New Life, a group that aimed at the improvement of society through the example of a community that would cultivate a perfect character in each of its members. At least one associate of the Fellowship advocated such things as rejecting possessions and leading a simple life characterised by manual labour, hand-woven woollen clothes, sandals, vegetarianism, and ultimately free sexual – indeed, homosexual – expression.[6] That Shaw was susceptible to some of these appeals, with regard to clothing and food at least, reminds us that both his fads and his socialism were parts of a wider quest for an alternative to the conventional ethics of his age. But the Fellowship's ideals were hardly likely to alter society at large in the near future. Some of its members, as Shaw later explained, 'modestly feeling that the revolution would have to wait an unreasonably long time if postponed till they personally had attained perfection, set up the banner of Socialism militant'.[7]

The banner was unfurled in January 1884, when the

Fabian Society was formed; in May, Shaw, attracted by the name, which suggested a group of educated people rather than the proletarians with whom he would have felt uneasy, went to a meeting; in September, he joined what was then only the second English socialist organisation; in January 1885, he was elected to the Fabian Executive and re-elected annually till he retired from it in 1911. In little over a year the remarkable group of early Fabians had gathered. Along with Shaw, the most significant of these was Sidney Webb, whose prodigious powers of research and command of fact were instrumental in establishing and supporting Fabian doctrine (after his marriage in 1892, much of Webb's sociological work was done jointly with his wife, Beatrice) and whose energies led him to an influential position on the London County Council, to the founding of the London School of Economics and *The New Statesman*, to Parliament, eventually to the dignity of being Lord Passfield, and finally – largely at Shaw's insistence – to burial in Westminster Abbey.

The most notorious of the group was undoubtedly Mrs Annie Besant, whose advocacy of atheism and birth control had brought about a much publicised trial. She was a beautiful woman and an even more compelling orator than Shaw himself, to whom she was much attracted. Shaw did not respond in kind; after a few years she deserted the Fabians for Theosophy. Most significant among the other early Fabians were Shaw's friend Graham Wallas, later an author and professor of political science, and Sidney Olivier, then a clerk in the Colonial Office like Webb, later Governor of Jamaica. The Society was to include such men as H. G. Wells, Bertrand Russell, and Clement Attlee, but in the crucial early years the central figures, along with the secretary, E. R. Pease, were Shaw, Webb, Wallas, and Oliver: D'Artagnan and the Three

Musketeers as Shaw called them, 'The Four', as they were known to other members.[8] Numbering only forty in 1885, the Fabians remained by preference a small group: there were 361 in 1891, and by the next year they were actually discouraging membership, not indulging 'in any vision of a Fabian army any bigger than stage army'.[9]

Convinced that Marxian economics were faulty and that an attempt at violent revolution would be futile, the Fabians were committed to the gradual achievement of socialism by constitutional means: their motto was 'educate, agitate, organise!' If they did relatively little organising, or even agitating, they managed an extraordinary amount of educating, ultimately making it 'as easy and matter-of-course for the ordinary respectable Englishman to be a Socialist as to be a Liberal or a Conservative'. (Shaw himself, though a lifelong Fabian, had occasional doubts as revealed, for example, in the Preface to the 1931 reprinting of the *Fabian Essays*. Claiming that at the end of the century the Fabians had convinced the workers that 'the greatest Socialist of that day, the poet and craftsman William Morris' – head of the rival Socialist League – was wrong to advocate revolution, he admitted with uncharacteristic hesitation, 'It is not so certain to-day as it seemed in the eighties that Morris was not right'.) The influence of the Fabians was spread by a remarkable range of activities. The Society produced an extensive body of writing, not only the works published by the individual members, but the long series of 'Tracts' on specific, largely domestic topics, for the Fabians were weak on foreign affairs, and the often reprinted *Fabian Essays* (Shaw wrote his last new Preface for it when he was over ninety), a lucid analysis of the social and economic bases for a gradual transition to socialism. Lectures and debates were to the Fabians both a means of educating themselves and disseminating their views: in 1888 the Society gave over seven hundred lectures, in 1892 over three thousand! The Fabians often invited outsiders to address them (Shaw even extended an invitation to one of his characters, the Reverend Morell of *Candida*), though they could be ruthless in the question period, one overly confident speaker being described in the press as having been 'Butchered to Make a Fabian Holiday'.

A peculiarly Fabian activity was 'Permeation', the anonymous insinuation of socialist ideas and programmes by writing for the more conservative press and especially by having Fabians join other political associations and move specific 'gas-and-water' proposals through their unsuspecting agency. These exploits of the then youthful Fabians had, in the words of William Irvine, something of 'the gay audacity and melodramatic resource of a college prank'.[10] The most celebrated of such permeations was perpetrated by Shaw who, having infiltrated the Executive of the South St Pancras Liberal and Radical Association, submitted to an obscure meeting the whole of a hypothetical Liberal Party programme concocted by Sidney Webb and, with the unwitting aid of the local parliamentary candidate, got it passed unanimously and immediately had it printed in a London newspaper 'with a report of an admirable speech . . . supposed to have been delivered' by the candidate. The next day the candidate found the 'National Liberal Club in an uproar at his revolutionary break-away', but the material became part of the Liberal Party's election programme in 1892, though to no one's surprise Gladstone ignored it after he came to power.[11]

Although the Fabians had called upon Socialists to organise themselves into a political party as early as 1886, thus angering Morris and other revolutionists and repeated the call after the Liberal betrayal of 1892, the leading Fabians were not by temperament inclined to this work. Shaw, more and more committed to his career as a playwright, refused invitations to stand for Parliament, and Webb, a scholar and skilful committeeman, chose for the time being to work on the London County Council and behind the political scenes. (In 1906 an attempt by H. G. Wells to enlarge greatly the membership of the Fabian Society and thus alter the nature of its influence was foiled, largely by Shaw's skill as a speaker and parliamentarian.) There were Fabians among the founders and early membership of the Labour Party, but its organisation was not a specifically Fabian activity. Indeed, Shaw came to feel that the Labour Party aimed less at establishing socialism than 'an oligarchy of trade unionists', and sixty years after the publication of the *Fabian Essays* he continued to insist that the Society 'must remain a minority of cultural snobs and genuinely scientific Socialist tacticians.'[12]

Shaw's later political views were marked by increasing distrust of the power of the mass electorate, 'mobocracy' as he called it, and, partly as a result, by the contorted effort to see in the dictators of the 1930s some qualities of the wise and competent ruler (a surrogate for the capable father he had never known), whom he had idealised as early as the Caesar of *Caesar and Cleopatra*. Shaw understood the dangers in the Fascists' 'romantic appetite for military glory', but he insisted on seeing Fascism essentially in economic terms, as little more than an alternative form of capitalism, superior to what he saw as the bankrupt liberal tradition ('the cry of Liberty is always on the lips of the propertied classes who own the lion's share of the land and capital and have nothing to fear but the nationalization of these resources') in that it trained citizens to look to the state 'instead of to their private individual competitive effort to make their lives tolerable.'[13] His attitude made Shaw disquietingly insensitive to dictatorial brutality, including of course Stalin's, even to the horrors of Hitler's genocidal antisemitism. Eric Bentley is kinder to Shaw than he need be in excusing Shaw's 'championing of the rightist against the liberal' as 'the old-fashioned devil's advocacy of a Victorian debater', but Bentley himself grants that 'to stress the dangers of liberalism when civilization is threatened by illiberalism is perhaps the most suspicious item in Shaw's long political career.'[14]

Less disquieting, but no less revealing, are two Shavian concerns that lead even beyond the boundaries of economics: idleness and equality of income. Although Shaw was well aware of the febrile demands of 'fashionable' life ('I would cheerfully peddle bootlaces rather than be condemned to it'), he was obsessed with any failure, but especially that of the wealthy, to do productive work. His term for this failure, 'idleness', may be the most insistently repeated word in his political writings, which champion not the lower classes against the upper but workers against idlers. 'We do not dream of allowing people to murder, kidnap, break into houses . . . ', Shaw fumes, 'yet we tolerate idling, which does more harm in one year than all the legally punishable crimes in the world in ten.'[15] Such denunciations, repeated again and again, derive not merely from the youthful Shaw's resentment of the reproaches of his mother and sister in the early London years (he 'disproves' their complaints by making them his own and directing them against another target), or from genuine anger at seeing the poor 'wasting their labor in providing service and luxuries for idle rich people', but from an ultimate Carlylean religious sense that one's work justifies one's life. (Compare, for example, Vivie Warren's 'salvation' through work in *Mrs Warren's Profession* with Hector Hushabye's 'damnation' through idleness in *Heartbreak House*.) To denounce idleness was for Shaw to affirm a belief in a kind of salvation through deeds.

An affirmation of a different order inheres in another persistent Shavian idea, first presented in a lecture to the Fabian Society in December of 1910, that absolute equality of income is the central necessity of socialist society. Although his view was taken up neither by the Fabians nor by communists in general, Shaw stuck to it, grudgingly admitting only late in life that it might be acceptable to raise workers' wages gradually till they reached the professional classes' level. After a series of socio-economic reasons for his proposal – for example, that it will force the nation to spend for 'necessaries first and luxuries last' – Shaw advances the argument that is for him the most important, the sexual one. Claiming that socialism is not being realised because 'the work is beyond the political capacity of the human animal as he exists today' and that to 'improve the nation' by breeding the Superman 'we must trust to nature: that is, to the fancies of our males and females', Shaw says that income must be equalised as the only way to abolish class and thus 'make the whole community intermarriageable.'[16] In this argument Shaw's economic and religious ideas are inextricably meshed. Equality of income is necessary not only to achieve a better society but to allow instinctive eugenics to raise mankind to a higher plane. In his commitment to this belief Shaw found his own version of salvation through faith.

But the personal faith that Shaw was working out through the 1890s, though related to his politics, was no mere extension of them. It was a teleological concept embracing the whole of creation, and seen in its light the great political and social cause to which he devoted so much of his vast energy became a comparatively trivial matter. The grand peroration to Section III of *The Revolutionist's Handbook*, for example, suggests, aside from Shaw's disabused sense of the motives of the proletariat, a view of humanity far transcending immediate economic aims:

> At certain moments there may even be a considerable material advance, as when the conquest of political power by the working class produces a better distribution of wealth through the simple action of the selfishness of the new masters; but all this is mere readjustment and reformation: until the heart and mind of the people is changed the very greatest man will no more dare to govern on the assumption that all are as great as he than a drover dare leave his flock to find its way through the streets as he himself would. Until there is an England in which every man is a Cromwell, a France in which every man is a Napoleon, a Rome in which every man is a Caesar, a Germany in which every man is a Luther plus a Goethe, the world will be no more improved by its heroes than a Brixton villa is improved by the pyramid of Cheops. The production of such nations is the only real change possible to us.

Though these ideas did not prevent Shaw from being the most practical and energetic of reformers, they were hardly calculated to draw enthusiastic assent from his socialist colleagues, particularly as, in Shaw's view, these fellow socialists had a vested interest in the reigning Darwinian orthodoxy that Shaw's Vitalist philosophy set out to oppose. Just as Darwinism had pleased *laissez-faire* capitalists by seeming to sanction economic competition as a law of nature and the rich and successful as the fittest to survive, it pleased socialists by implying that, as environment was a decisive influence on the life of an organism, so it was with society, which had to be reformed before one could expect change in the individual. Thus, in disputing Darwinism, Shaw said that 'even in Socialist Societies which existed solely to substitute the law of fellowship for the law of competition, and the method of providence and wisdom for the method of rushing violently down a steep place into the sea, I found myself regarded as a blasphemer and an ignorant sentimentalist. . . .'[17] But despite the disapprobation of his fellows, Shaw's religion remained deeply enmeshed with his politics, encouraging him, for example, to argue after World War I that the 'highly civilized Western Powers' (which he held to be at a more advanced evolutionary stage) should have formed an alliance 'against the primitive tyrannies of the East'.[18]

The point here is not the curious (to a post-colonial sensibility) rationalising of cultural ethnocentricity but the degree to which Shaw's political thinking was impregnated by his religious concepts. Their persistent congruence derives from their common roots in Shaw's evolutionary vision. For Shaw, existence had to be seen as part of a continuing process in which individual gratification was of little account but for which individual effort was absolutely essential. Just as a part of Shaw's impatience with Marxism lay in its insistence on the mechanical inevitability of the historical process (there was no doubt that the interplay of economic forces would lead to the triumph of the proletariat), similarly much of his distaste for Darwinism derived from its portrayal of evolutionary development as independent of any volition, as entirely lacking a vital impulse.

Despite his profound spiritual inclinations, Shaw was able to accept with pleasure the modern geology that in opening up vast stretches of historic time had swept aside as antiquated rubbish the traditional, Biblical, 'creationist' doctrine that had postulated a beginning for the world in 4004 BC, according to the chronology of Archbishop Ussher, along with the simultaneous origin of the various species of animals and the separate creation of mankind. Shaw rejoiced in the evolutionist view not only because of its scientific truth but because it seemed to destroy the last possibility of belief in the 'nursery bogey' God of the Old Testament – Shelley's 'Almighty Fiend' and Blake's 'Nobodaddy' were terms Shaw borrowed – who had 'a petty character and unlimited power' and was 'spiteful, cruel, jealous, vindictive, and physically violent'. (Nor was Shaw much more patient with the pieties of the New Testament, universal love and forgiveness of sins seeming to his lucid puritanism as egregious sentimentality and utter moral irresponsibility.)[19] But the positive achievements of the evolutionary view of history were, in Shaw's mind, counterbalanced by what he saw as the horrifying negations of the Darwinian theory of Natural Selection – or as Shaw, considering it highly unnatural, preferred to call it, Circumstantial Selection.

The notion that evolutionary development had proceeded by the mindless mechanism of the 'survival of the fittest', by the accidental perpetuation of whatever characteristics happened at a given moment to respond best to the Malthusian pressures of population and food supply, was to Shaw an intolerable rejection of all spirituality and ultimately all meaning. Happy to be rid of the Old Testament 'anthropomorphic idol', Shaw might have said with Nietzsche, 'God is dead', but he could never have accepted the implied denial of all divine significance

in the universe, and it was this denial that he saw in
Darwinism:

> But when its whole significance dawns on you, your
> heart sinks into a heap of sand within you. There is a
> hideous fatalism about it, a ghastly and damnable
> reduction of beauty and intelligence, of strength and
> purpose, of honor and aspiration, to such casually
> picturesque changes as an avalanche may make in a
> mountain landscape, or a railway accident in a human
> figure. To call this Natural Selection is a blasphemy,
> possible to many for whom Nature is nothing but a
> casual aggregation of inert and dead matter, but
> eternally impossible to the spirits and souls of the
> righteous. If it be no blasphemy, but a truth of science,
> then the stars of heaven, the showers and dew, the
> winter and summer, the fire and heat, the mountains and
> hills, may no longer be called on to exalt the Lord with
> us by praise: their work is to modify all things by blindly
> starving and murdering everything that is not lucky
> enough to survive in the universal struggle for hogwash.[20]

The impassioned commitment to such familiar values as
beauty and honour (as opposed to mere aestheticism and
gentility, embodied, for instance, in Apollodorus and
Britannus of *Caesar and Cleopatra*), the exalted vision of
man and nature united in a spiritual purpose, and the
anger at the denial of such a purpose (expressed in the
brutally colloquial 'hogwash' at the rhetorical climax) all
reveal, behind the debater and the wit, the man who never
tired of quoting the complaint of his mentor Samuel
Butler, that Darwin had 'banished mind from the
universe', for to Shaw that meant he had banished spirit
and purpose as well.

If Shaw rejected both Darwinian science and traditional religion, where was he to find an alternative? An answer is that he did not quite find one. Shaw's habit of playful oratorical hyberbole often makes him sound as if he had created as an alternative an all-embracing philosophical and theological system, but such was not the case. Profound as was his revulsion from the mechanical aspects of Darwinism, Shaw granted that it was one of the modes through which evolution worked and that his denial of its exclusivity was not a 'truth of science' but an act of faith. 'When a man tells you that you are a product of Circumstantial Selection solely,' he wrote, 'you cannot finally disprove it. You can only tell him out of the depths of your inner conviction that he is a fool and a liar.' Moreover, what Shaw produced out of the depths of his own inner conviction was not a thorough and comprehensive Vitalist system – such as that which, drawing on Shaw, C. E. M. Joad attempted in *Matter, Life and Value* – but a selective discourse that was at once passionate and playful, a teleological vision, a dramatised mythology. It served its purpose by allowing Shaw to live and to write, by helping to hold at bay the tragic sense of life that hovers behind the façade of Shavian comedy. Though Shaw's Vitalist ideas are most explicit in *Man and Superman* and *Back to Methuselah*, they permeate all his works, and it is important to see their nature and something of their origins.

Although Shaw found bits and pieces of ideas useful to him in the works of an extraordinary variety of thinkers and writers, the one to whom he was most profoundly indebted was undoubtedly Samuel Butler, whose posthumous fame as the author of *The Way of All Flesh* was due in considerable part to Shaw's praise of him in the Preface to *Major Barbara* as 'in his own department the greatest English writer of the latter half of the XIX century'. Butler was significant to Shaw for his 'earnest and constant sense of the importance of money', for his disabused vision of the family, and especially for his views as a Darwinian controversialist. The most persistent of Butler's remarkable range of artistic and intellectual interests was his anti-Darwinism, with which Shaw became acquainted as early as 1887, when he reviewed *Luck or Cunning?* for the *Pall Mall Gazette*. Making little effect on the general public or the scientific community, though his analysis of Darwin's stylistic obscurantism was mercilessly penetrating, Butler pursued through a series of volumes the argument that Charles Darwin's view of the mechanism of evolution was erroneous and that a more nearly correct view had been advocated by such earlier evolutionists as Charles's grandfather, Dr Erasmus Darwin, and the French naturalists Buffon and Lamarck, most explicitly the last, whose impressive titles (Chevalier de Lamarck, Professor of Zoology at the Museum of Natural History) are amiably discarded by Shaw, who presents him as 'a French soldier named Lamarck, who had beaten his musket into a microscope and turned zoologist'.

As early as 1879 in *Evolution, Old and New* Butler, a gifted translator whose slyly ironic rendering of *The Odyssey* may have helped shape Shaw's colloquial treatment of history, had made parts of Lamarck's work conveniently available. In an important passage Lamarck argues that the 'common origins of bodily and mental phenomena' had not been recognised because study had concentrated on man, the most complex organism, instead of working up from the simpler ones. Proceeding in this way, he continues, we 'should have seen that sense of needs – originally hardly perceptible, but gradually increasing in intensity and variety – has led to the attempt to gratify them; that actions thus induced, having become habitual and energetic, have occasioned the development of organs adapted for their performance; that the force which excites organic movement . . . was . . . introduced into the animals themselves, and fixed within them; and lastly that it gave rise to sensibility and, in the end, to intelligence'.[21] Although Butler, along with Shaw, felt that 'the force' was always in the organisms, he saw that the crucial element here was the concept of change proceeding from a 'sense of needs', an active desire on the part of the organism, rather than from blind chance. Latent in this passage is much in Shaw: not only his whimsical vision at the end of *Back to Methuselah* of the Ancients developing various extra organs as a kind of experimental hobby and his serious one of intelligence as the climax of the evolutionary process but his profounder sense of that development as being progressive, purposive, and willed.

Once the Lamarckian idea of evolution as a continuous striving impelled by a force ultimately within the organism had been accepted, there was a refuge for such religious sensibilities as Shaw's and Butler's from despair at the emptiness of the mechanistic Darwinian universe, for God himself could be seen as the great creative force, 'an incorporeal Purpose, unable to do anything directly, but mysteriously able to create corporeal organs and agents to accomplish that purpose, which, as far as we can see, is the attainment of infinite wisdom and infinite power', as Shaw put it in the 'Postscript: After Twentyfive Years' to *Back to Methuselah*'. This Shavian view of the Divinity derives with little alteration from Butler's conception as expressed, for example, in this passage from *Evolution, Old and New*:

Shall we see God henceforth as embodied in all living

45

forms; as dwelling in them; as being that power in them whereby they have learnt to fashion themselves, each one according to its ideas of its own convenience, and to make itself not only a microcosm, or little world, but a little unwritten history of the universe from its own point of view into the bargain? From everlasting, in time past, only in so far as life has lasted; invisible only in so far as the ultimate connection between the will to do and the thing which does is invisible; imperishable, only in so far as life as a whole is imperishable; omniscient and omnipotent, within the limits only of a very long and large experience, but ignorant and impotent in respect of all else – limited in all the above respects, yet even so incalculably vaster than anything that we can conceive?[22]

When Shaw has Major Barbara resolve, near the end of her play, to do God's work for its own sake, 'the work he had to create us to do because it cannot be done except by living men and women', we catch a momentary glimpse of the God of Butler, 'ignorant and impotent' outside of the range of his own creatures' experience, forced to enter into 'living forms' to create the future. (John Stuart Mill had already postulated a Deity who had, as he put it in 'Theism', one of the *Three Essays on Religion*, 'great wisdom without the power of foreseeing and calculating everything', and in whose universe evil was caused by 'errors of Creative Force'; Butler presents a concept different from Mill's by suggesting in place of a designer external to his creation one who is 'embodied in all living forms', the organs through which he must work; evil, for Shaw as a Butlerian thinker, is less a mistake by the Creative Force than a necessary part of its trial-and-error process.)[23]

The problem with Lamarck's view of the process of

change lay in his alluring, much disputed assertion that acquired characteristics were inherited, 'that Nature conserves in offspring all that their life and environment has developed in parents'.[24] Butler's essential contribution as a biological theorist is the working out in *Life and Habit* of a complex, closely reasoned hypothesis of just how acquired characteristics were, in fact, passed on to later generations. This was the doctrine of 'unconscious memory', the notion that the instinctive habits of an organism (digesting food, for example, or growing feathers in the case of a bird) are memories of similar actions performed by its ancestors and transmitted through the generations by the literal physical continuity of the species. In a striking passage from his book *Unconscious Memory* Butler writes, 'if a man of eighty may consider himself identical with the baby from whom he has developed, so that he may say, "I am the person who at six months old did this or that", then the baby may just as fairly claim identity with its father and mother, and say to its parents on being born, "I was you only a few months ago". By parity of reasoning each living form now on earth must be able to claim identity with each generation of its ancestors up to the primordial cell inclusive'.[25] Thus habits acquired at any point in the evolutionary chain – perhaps by use, as in the celebrated instance of the giraffe's stretching its neck – could be passed on to its descendants. It is essentially this Butlerian argument, that evolutionary development consists of the transmission of acquired characteristics through unconscious memory, that Shaw so exuberantly recapitulates, most specifically in the section 'How Acquirements Are Inherited' in the Preface to *Back to Methuselah*:

You are alive; and you want to be more alive. You want

an extension of consciousness and of power. You want, consequently, additional organs: that is, additional habits. You get them because you want them badly enough to keep trying for them until they come. Nobody knows how: nobody knows why: all we know is that the thing actually takes place. We relapse miserably from effort to effort until the old organ is modified or the new one created, when suddenly the impossible becomes possible and the habit is formed.

Butler himself had put it no less eloquently or mystically, writing, 'living forms grow gradually but persistently into physical conformity with their own intentions, and become outward and visible signs of the inward and spiritual faith, or wants of faith, that have been most within them'.[26]

Although Lamarck emphasised the organism's reaction to changed circumstances, Butler insisted that his predecessor had made 'in effect . . . effort, intention, will . . . underlie progress in organic development'.[27] For Shaw too the vital will was central to his vision, and he looked beyond Butler for support, finding it in a number of figures, among them Schopenhauer, 'that very freethinking philosopher . . . who re-established the old theological doctrine that reason is no motive power; that the true motive power in the world is will (otherwise Life)'.[28] For Schopenhauer's ultimate claim that the will led one into unsatisfiable desires and that escape from life dominated by its incessant demands was to be sought, Shaw had only contempt, denouncing it as an 'idiotic pessimist conclusion', even though there is, as we shall see, a darker, generally repressed aspect of his temper more sympathetic to such a claim than he allowed himself to acknowledge. In addition, Shaw rallied to his cause Schopenhauer's mentor, Goethe himself. In the Hell scene of *Man and Superman* Shaw allows Don Juan, as part of his ironic praise of the Devil's establishment, to play with the final lines of *Faust*, translating 'Das Unbeschreibliche/Hier ist's getan' (The indescribable/ Here is it acted out) into the Shavian 'the poetically nonsensical here is good sense' and follows Goethe's 'The Eternal Feminine draws us ever upward and on' with Don Juan's denigrating 'without getting us a step further'. But in *Back to Methuselah* he is far from using Goethe to make fun of romantic attitudes. Here 'Goethe is Olympian' because unlike other playwrights he is an evolutionist; he is praised as Poet-Scientist who had divined the truth of evolution (some of Goethe's scientific work did, in fact, contribute to evolutionary theory), and his Eternal Feminine is hailed as 'the first modern manifesto of the mysterious force in creative evolution'.

Whether, or to what degree, Shaw is here claiming an influence or an affinity is difficult to say. It is, in any case, more important to recognise that Shaw's ideas are part of a great intellectual current of historical-religious speculation flowing through the nineteenth century. For example, the idea that the whole of humanity in its progress through history constitutes a kind of divine being that one may enter into and thus become one with the Deity, is central not only to Shaw's thought but to that of the French Positivist philosopher Auguste Comte. At least one study of Shaw's intellectual background argues for a specific Comtian influence (from the house on Fitzroy Square where Shaw and his mother lived for several years it was only a modest stroll across Bloomsbury to an English Positivist 'temple'); whether or not there is such an influence, the significant point is that Comte and Shaw were part of a wide-ranging effort to reconcile the ancient desires for religion with the new attitudes created by the discoveries of science.[29]

With the work of another French thinker, Henri Bergson, there is clearly a connection, for Shaw appropriated from Bergson and thereafter regularly used the term 'Creative Evolution' to designate his pattern of beliefs. But Bergson's *Creative Evolution* did not appear until 1907, by which time *Man and Superman* had been written and Shaw's ideas substantially formed. Undoubtedly Shaw was pleased with the congruence between his notion of the Life Force sweeping through history and triumphing over matter and Bergson's concept of the *élan vital*; it may indeed have been to some extent Bergson's prestige that tempted Shaw to make the now hollow declaration that Creative Evolution was 'the religion of the twentieth century'. (Bergson, however, was less than pleased when, at a luncheon in his honour in London, he heard Shaw present to the gathering an exposition of what purported to be Bergson's philosophy. When Bergson interrupted, 'Ah, no-o! It is not qvite zat!', Shaw replied, 'Oh, my dear fellow, I understand your philosophy much better than you do' and, despite Bergson's annoyance, continued cheerfully with his discourse.)[30] But even the crucial speculation that life may overcome death, which Shaw shares with Bergson, is presented by Shaw as the overcoming of an outworn 'habit', a term that links it conclusively to Butler.

This idea, dramatised in *Back to Methuselah*, of vastly extended, ultimately boundless life is Shaw's final visionary transcending of human limitations, but he had postulated a somewhat different means to this end in his previous 'metabiological' drama, *Man and Superman*. Here again caution is required in assessing influence. When the idea of the Superman appears – and it does so

only briefly – at the end of the Hell scene, it is identified by
the Devil in a characteristic Shavian whimsy as the product
of a 'German Polish madman' named Nietzsche, as being
'as old as Prometheus', and as having already been
embodied in Wagner's Siegfried, all of which considerably
blurs its meaning. Even Ana's final appeal to the universe,
'a father for the Superman', is only a generalised
expression of longing. Perhaps the statue is wisest in
assessing the word as simply a war cry; 'a good cry', as he
says, 'is half the battle'. In *The Revolutionist's Handbook*
Shaw grants that we 'do not know what sort of man' is
wanted as Superman to surpass the mere cliché of the
'goodlooking philosopher-athlete', and the grotesquerie of
his project for eugenic breeding suggests the desperation of
his quest for 'a more highly evolved animal' than man.
However, Shaw's curious eugenic speculation that a robust
British country squire and an 'intellectual, highly civilized
Jewess' might produce a son superior to both is
Nietzschean, being lifted almost intact from *Beyond Good
and Evil*. Shaw must have been particularly taken with
a passage in Nietzsche such as the following, which
suggests that the Superman is a stage in evolutionary
progress: 'What is the ape to men? A laughing stock
or a painful embarrassment. And just so shall man be
to the Superman: a laughing-stock or a painful
embarrassment'.[31] But Nietzsche, whose historical and
artistic judgements Shaw called 'professorial folly', saw
the Superman as a personal efflorescence; Shaw, despite
his admiration for such 'accidental' Supermen as
Shakespeare, Goethe, and Shelley, looked forward to the
universal elevation of mankind and to the utter abnegation
of the self.

It was this impulse that Shaw dramatised in one of the
few touching moments to be found in the largely arid

stretches of the *Back to Methuselah* plays. At the end of *Tragedy of an Elderly Gentleman* the leading character begs to be allowed to stay with those who have achieved long life and not be forced back to the ludicrous hypocrisies of the 'normal' world. 'I cannot live among people to whom nothing is real. . . . If I go back I shall die of disgust and despair'. A moment later he is granted a merciful death. To preserve himself, and his art, from such lurking 'disgust and despair' Shaw needed even more than the sweetness and vitality of his humorous vision; he needed not so much a viable system of ideas as a philosophic metaphor through which man could be seen as redeemed from the flesh and the iniquities of his nature. To this end he created the remarkable circular myth that he partly dramatised in *Back to Methuselah* and summarised in its concluding speech by Lilith, an ultimate feminine embodiment of the Life Force. She had 'sundered' herself to produce Adam and Eve who, unable to endure immortality, had accepted death but whose descendants were in the end the Ancients of the last play, about to become immortal, immaterial, omnipotent, omniscient – in effect, gods: 'after passing a million goals they press on to the goal of redemption from the flesh, to the vortex freed from matter, to the whirlpool in pure intelligence that, when the world began, was a whirlpool in pure force'. Lilith resolves to allow them to continue, though she knows that 'they shall become one with me and supersede me'; in the 'vast domain' of the universe 'as yet unbearably desert, my seed shall one day fill it and master its matter to its uttermost confines'. In this image the seed has become one with the mother/force and, filling the womb of space, the embryo/god has achieved all that it can imagine.

But neither this briefly glimpsed fantasy nor the more

explicit political and religious ideas so richly woven into the texture of Shaw's plays constitute a full explanation of his work. If we are to understand Shaw, we must know not only his mind but his art. We must see in what relationship he stood to the theatre of his age and how, out of its often commonplace materials, he constructed the dazzling edifice of his drama.

3
The Life of the Theatre: Shakespeare, Wagner, Ibsen and the Theatre of the Age

Most realistic plays of any ambition written in the twentieth century have been – more or less – like the plays of Ibsen or like the plays of Chekhov. That is to say they have been, if Ibsenite, firm in structure, decisive in characterisation, and often focused on questions of public morality; if Chekhovian, they have been freer, more episodic in structure, comparatively ambiguous in characterisation, and focused on private, psycho-sexual concerns. This over-simplification may beg to be refuted, or at least qualified because it is unjust to the complexity of the modern theatre and reductive of the two great masters whose names are here appropriated, but not on the grounds that it ignores a notable comic tradition deriving from the work of Bernard Shaw. No such tradition, after all, exists. It is extraordinary that the other two initial masters of modern drama should be so profoundly influential that, at least arguably, subsequent plays have been in modes delineated by their work, whereas Shaw remains a solitary giant, in art as in life childless.

That the sound of Shavian laughter should evoke no echoes appears at first curious. The matter of Shaw's drama was ostensibly so public, the style so ingratiating, his success, though long delayed, so glittering when it came that imitation, even the development of a school, would seem to have been a matter of course. But in fact even a brief consideration of the peculiar temper of Shaw's work suggests a number of reasons for its having remained, quite literally, inimitable. First of all, there is the question, already considered, of Shaw's heterodox opinions. Even those plays that do not offer occasions for arguing economic questions or explicating the doctrine of Creative Evolution inevitably reflect his social and religious ideas. In the nature of things, significant numbers of West End or Broadway playwrights have not tended to combine a passionate and knowledgeable commitment to socialism with a private, mystical vision of the universe.

Moreover, beyond this special set of intellectual convictions, Shaw brought to the theatre an exuberant humour that was not only unparalleled in its vivacity and endless inventiveness but, considering his antagonistic relationship with the capitalist world, astonishing in its sweetness. One might have expected the exiled Irish writer to portray bourgeois English society with Swiftian harshness, but he produced instead a body of comic portraiture that takes its coloration from the brighter pages of Dickens and Molière. And to make these portraits speak he invented a unique dramatic rhetoric: operatic in its control of voices and rhythms, aria-like in the luxurious length of its grand speeches, confidently oratorical in the balance of its cadences. Nothing like it has been heard since, because no writer has come to the theatre after a similar immersion in music and public declamation.[1]

Finally, Shaw stood in a special relationship to the theatre of the early modern age, one which has ceased to be possible for later playwrights. Although Shaw was a tireless advocate of the new realistic drama – primarily demarcated by the work of Ibsen and Chekhov – he did not himself write this kind of drama. Poised as he was at a peculiar instant in dramatic history, the last moment at which the old drama of the nineteenth century remained viable, he was led by his theatrical instincts, especially in the first flush of his newly-found powers, to play on the old themes the final possible variation: to present them in such a way that they would at once be themselves and a parodistic inversion of themselves.

But before considering the use Shaw made of the theatre of his time, it is important to understand more clearly his relation to it. The reviews he wrote as a drama critic are revelatory, whether he was commenting on good plays or bad; no less important are his championing of Henrik Ibsen, admired as the greatest of contemporary dramatists, his explication of Wagner – venerated as the musico-dramatic master of the preceding generation – and his long continued 'love-hate' relationship with the master whose shadow darkened, as Shaw felt, the English theatrical landscape – William Shakespeare.

The *locus classicus* of Shaws confrontation with Shakespeare is 'Blaming the Bard', his review of Sir Henry Irving's production of *Cymbeline* in September of 1896.[2] He began by denouncing the play as 'for the most part stagey trash of the lowest melodramatic order, in parts abominably written . . . and, judged in point of thought by modern intellectual standards, vulgar, foolish, offensive, indecent, and exasperating beyond all tolerance'. After further denunciation of Shakespeare's 'monstrous rhetorical fustian, his unbearable platitudes', Shaw indulges himself in a splendid crescendo of vanity: 'With the single exception of Homer, there is no eminent writer, not even Sir Walter Scott, whom I can despise so entirely as I despise Shakespear [Shaw avoided the conventional spelling] when I measure my mind against his'. Having perpetrated the supreme literary impiety, Shaw proceeds to surpass it in a climax of mischievous irony: 'To read *Cymbeline* and to think of Goethe, of Wagner, of Ibsen, is for me, to imperil the habit of studied moderation of statement which years of public responsibility as a journalist have made almost second nature in me'. Behind its vertiginous comic fantasy, this statement means exactly what it says, which is not that Shaw disliked Shakespeare. He called himself, in fact, 'an ardent Shakespearean' described *Twelfth Night* as an 'exquisite poem', rejoiced in Forbes-Robertson's *Hamlet* because so much of the text had been retained, and – in the paragraph following the passage above – granted that Shakespeare 'has outlasted thousands of abler thinkers' and has 'enormous power over language' and a 'prodigious fund' of 'vital energy'. (Shaw did not, however, admire Shakespeare's contemporaries, describing even Marlowe as 'the true Elizabethan blank verse beast'.)

This ardent Shakespearean's attack on the mindless bardolatry of both audiences and performers had a serious purpose. In a letter to Ellen Terry (27 January 1897), part of his campaign to convince her she should act in his plays, he wrote, 'The theatre is my battering ram as much as the platform or the press . . . My capers are part of a bigger design than you think: Shakespere, for instance, is to me one of the towers of the Bastille, and down he must come'. Annoyed by the critical praise for the textually mutilated, picture-frame stagings of Shakespeare offered by the West End managers (Shaw admired the platform-stage performances of the Elizabethan Stage Society) and infuriated by the critical denunciation of Ibsen, the leader of the new drama, Shaw, 'among the most bardolatrous of all the bardolators', felt 'that it was necessary to debunk Shakespeare as well as extol Ibsen'.[3]

But the Shaw whose perceptive comments on Shakespeare fill the Preface to *The Dark Lady of the Sonnets*, itself written as an appeal for public funds to endow the Shakespeare Theatre at Stratford, and whose characterisation of Shakespeare in that Preface is an idealised portrait of himself, nevertheless found Shakespeare a disquieting presence. He was particularly troubled by those plays whose crucial characters seemed to him 'only pessimists and railers'. Lacking a kind of 'negative capability', Shaw could not forgive Shakespeare for failing to offer a systematic, optimistic vision of human life and history, what Shaw called a religion. In the 'Evolution in the Theatre' section of the Preface to *Back to Methuselah*, he wrote that Shakespeare 'forced himself in among the greatest of playwrights without having once entered that region in which Michael Angelo, Beethoven, Goethe, and the antique Athenian stage poets are great. He would not really be great at all if it were not that he had religion enough to be aware that his religionless condition was one of despair'. This tangled passage suggests less about Shakespeare than about the need to deal with the ultimate dilemmas of existence that lurk behind the brilliant façade of much of the Shavian drama; Shaw's solution, however, was not the direct confrontation of the Shakespearean tragedies nor even solely the creation of his optimistic teleology but, as the study of his plays will suggest, the dramatising of various modes of withdrawal that allow certain favoured characters, from Vivie Warren to Saint Joan, to remove themselves from the limitations of human existence to a realm of higher, if more severe gratification. Though a bardolator to the end, Shaw could never quite be reconciled to the tragic Shakespeare who dealt with despair by strategies so different from his own.

He might well have had similar reservations with regard to his admired Wagner, who fancied himself the heir of Schopenhauer's pessimism. However, Shaw was able to evade them by two quite distinct devices: creative interpretation and unconscious absorption. When Shaw reflected Wagnerian elements in his own plays, usually without recognising them, they were associated with the darker, more private aspects of his own temperament, but in his public interpretation, *The Perfect Wagnerite*, first issued in 1898, Shaw delighted in offering Wagner as an exponent of socialism and even (before the presentation of his own ideas in *Man and Superman*) of Creative Evolution. Making much of Wagner's involvement in the Dresden uprisings of 1849 and his association with the anarchist Bakunin, Shaw insisted that *The Ring of the Nibelungen* – or rather *The Niblung's Ring*, for he blithely Anglicised most of the names – was a kind of socialist allegory 'and really demanded modern costumes, tall hats for Tarnhelms, factories for Nibelheims, villas for Valhallas, and so on. . . .'[4] In this scheme the brutal, greedy 'Alberic' ('such dwarfs are quite common in London') in stealing the 'Rhine gold' acquires the capitalist's power to make 'his fellow-creatures . . . slave miserably overground and underground, lashed to their work by the invisible whip of starvation'. Among the articles produced in Alberic's mine, or capitalist enterprise ('it might just as well be a match factory, with yellow phosphorus, phossy jaw, a large dividend, and plenty of clergymen shareholders'), is the magic tarnhelm. 'This helmet is a very common article in our streets, where it generally takes the form of a tall hat. It makes a man invisible as a shareholder, and changes him into various shapes, such as a pious Christian, a subscriber to hospitals . . . a shrewd, practical, independent Englishman, and what not, when he is really a pitiful parasite on the commonwealth. . . .'.

Opposed to the 'savage' concept of life involving only money, power, and personal satisfaction is the higher thought of 'the establishment of a social order founded on common bonds of moral faith'. However, according to Shaw, when Wotan attempts to realise such a higher type of civilisation, he finds that he must be 'crowned Pontiff and King', that he must construct Valhalla, the 'mighty fortress . . . church-castle', and that he thus becomes entangled in and corrupted by the laws of church and state. To escape his dilemma Wotan conceives of a Hero, one of a race that can 'deliver the world and himself from his limited powers and disgraceful bargains', a 'creature in whom the god's unavailing thought shall have become effective will and life. . . .'.

At this point Shaw, in effect, shifts symbolic gears from the economic mode to the religious, beginning to use the language that he will often turn to in his later disquisitions on Creative Evolution. Here he describes Wotan's resolution that Erda, the First Mother, who is clearly an anticipation of Lilith in *Back to Methuselah*, shall produce a race of heroes: 'The life that came from her has ever climbed up to a higher and higher organization'. Sliding whimsically from one mode to the other, Shaw describes

Siegfried, the Hero, as 'a totally unmoral person, a born anarchist, the ideal of Bakoonin [whose name is rather phoneticised than Anglicised], an anticipation of the "overman" of Nietzsche'. However, Shaw can only carry his allegory to a certain point. Once Siegfried has thrust aside the Old Order in the person of Wotan and gone through the magic fire to 'Brynhild', Shaw can do nothing with the ecstasy of the lovers and the subsequent intrigues, dismissing the end of the tetralogy as 'mere' opera, conceived before Wagner's full commitment to socialism and scored after his disillusion with it.

But the Wagnerian influence, in the handling of sexual and familial relations rather than politics, thrusts its way uninvited into Shaw's own drama. Shaw himself acknowledged its presence in *Candida* by later claiming that when Marchbanks, who has, as Candida says, 'learnt to live without happiness', leaves at the end of the play, he goes out into 'Tristan's holy night'.[5] In asserting the superiority of the poet's realm, Shaw seems hardly to notice that he is equating it with the world of death, the true 'heil'ge Nacht' of Wagner's lovers, and he may even have been unaware that he was echoing the ending of *Candida* in a melancholy passage from 'The Valkyrie' section of *The Perfect Wagnerite*, written four years later, in which he describes how Wotan brings up Siegmund 'and teaches him the only power a god can teach, the power of doing without happiness'.

The disdaining of common existence by one who is the servant of a higher purpose – that of the Life Force, Shaw would say – is a pervasive, though often submerged theme in Shaw's work. It appears, for example, in another suprisingly 'Wagnerian' play, *Caesar and Cleopatra*. The story of a noble warrior who comes over the waters and rescues a royal but childlike maiden surrounded by threatening enemies, whatever its relations to the history of Caesar in Egypt, derives ultimately, though no doubt unconsciously, from *Lohengrin*, which begins with the same circumstances. Indeed, Caesar's first words, the speech to the Sphinx in which he claims that they have both entered the world from a happier place and that he has wandered 'seeking the lost regions from which my birth into this world exiled me . . . the home from which we have strayed' is noticeably reminiscent of Lohengrin's first words to his 'beloved swan' as he sends it back to the mystic realm from which it has brought him, 'Kehr' wieder nur zu unserm Glück!' [Return but to our happiness].[6] However, the central element linking these works is not the motif of the lost homeland but the failure of the royal maiden to live up to the exalted spiritual demands, actual or implied, of the rescuing warrior. Just as Elsa's possessiveness leads her to break her agreement not to ask her rescuer's name (it is the symbol of the inviolate self; to know it, is to destroy the bearer's power), so Cleopatra, growing to passionate maturity (she is 'the most dangerous of all Caesar's conquests'), in having Pothinus murdered takes upon herself Caesar's own 'powers of life and death'. As Lohengrin must retreat to the realm of the Grail, so Caesar must return to Rome and his death. Shaw found here in Wagner an exemplary image of the retreat from worldly entanglements that was to be a significant element in his own work.

This ambiguous attitude toward emotive, quasi-sexual relations appears in a more explicitly familial context in the play that is in the Shavian canon the analogue to Wagner's *Ring, Major Barbara*. Shaw himself suggests the connection between these works in the material he added to *The Perfect Wagnerite* in 1907, the year he published *Major Barbara*: in a playful exposition of pseudo-

Wagnerian economics he says that Alberich, in whose capitalist enterprises Fafner has had to invest his treasure, has been forced to make 'an earthly Providence for masses of workmen, creating towns, and governing markets'. The evocation of Undershaft is unmistakable here and in a passage immediately following on power exercised by commerce over Parliament and the press. There is, moreover, a hint at Cusins' role in the subsequent assertion that the 'end cannot come until Siegfried learns Alberic's trade and shoulders Alberic's burden'. In the working out of this material, however, Shaw's dramatic instinct guides him to recognise not Alberich, the Niebelheim dwarf, but Wotan, the commander of a mighty citadel, as the equivalent to Undershaft. It is, after all, Wotan who, like Undershaft, arranges for his succession by an 'orphan' hero who is also to possess his daughter. But these hero/rivals are ambiguous in their attitudes to the noble 'warrior' maidens toward whom they are so profoundly drawn: Cusins is 'intensely afraid' of marriage; Siegfried finds that it is Brünnhilde 'die hat ihn das Fürchten gelehrt' [who has taught him fear]. Even more problematic are the fathers' relationships with their daughters, who are extensions of themselves (Brünnhilde is Wotan's 'Wille'; Undershaft says, 'I shall hand on my torch to my daughter') and yet rebellious. Both fathers are remote or severe, yet protective: Sieglinde receives a sword, Brünnhilde fire, Barbara money. The daughters are loved but punished for challenging their fathers (Wotan removes Brünnhilde's godhead, Undershaft Barbara's faith in the army and thus her divine mission), and finally both daughters make a kind of peace with the parental powers. Far more deeply attuned to the psychological resonances of Wagner's myth than his politicising of it suggests, Shaw sensed in *The Ring* motifs a feeling closely allied to his tangled familial concerns and created from it his own curiously allusive masterpiece.

Shaw's relationship to his other revered nineteenth-century master dramatist ran a somewhat similar course. Although he produced a highly individualistic public explication of Ibsen, in his own work Shaw echoes his great predecessor in subtle and quite different ways. The notion that Shaw betrayed Ibsen by presenting him as a socialist is by now a critical commonplace, although it is not true. (Ibsen, who sympathised with the left despite his stern independence, was represented as being angered by what he heard of Shaw's presentation – in fact, he was not displeased by it – and Shaw earnestly asked Archer to rectify the matter when he saw Ibsen.) Nevertheless, socialist politics were influential in the making of what eventually became *The Quintessence of Ibsenism*. The book began as a long lecture by Shaw to the Fabian Society in July of 1890, part of a series on 'Socialism in Contemporary Literature' designed to keep the Society active through the summer. Shaw used the occasion, at least in part, to attack those abstract, uncompromising socialists who opposed the gradualism and emphasis on practical reforms of the Fabians. In his letter to Archer of 17 August asking him to clarify the lecture to Ibsen, he told Archer to explain that 'an eminent socialist critic made his plays the text for a fierce attack on the idealist section of the English Social Democrats, comparing them and their red flag to Hilmar Tonnesen and his "banner of the ideal"'.[7]

Addressing an audience interested primarily in social philosophy, Shaw, who had not yet begun his career as a playwright, set out not to examine the plays as complex artworks, but to present an exposition of 'Ibsenism'.

Society, Shaw argues, to conceal from itself unpleasant realities covers them with masks, or 'ideals', such as the notion of the beauty and holiness of love and family life to mask the brutality of sexual appetite and the necessities of social obligations. In the 'Ideals and Idealists' section of *The Quintessence* Shaw writes, 'We call this sort of fancy picture an Ideal; and the policy for forcing individuals to act on the assumption that all ideals are real, and to recognize and accept such action as standard moral conduct, absolutely valid under all circumstances, contrary conduct or any advocacy of it being discountenanced and punished as immoral, may therefore be described as the policy of idealism'. The most dangerous element in society, Shaw argues, is not the ordinary, well-meaning Philistine who amiably and thoughtlessly accepts things as they are but the 'idealist', the person who in his heart feels the falsity of conventional ideas and institutions but, frightened by this recognition, all the more desperately affirms their truth and sanctity. Only the true pioneer, the 'realist' such as Shelley or Ibsen, dares to discard current pieties, to struggle for a new and genuine ideal, and to face being reviled as cynic and immoralist.

When Shaw applies his concept to Ibsen's plays from *Brand* onward, the results are always intriguing, sometimes illuminating, occasionally peculiar. A persistent distortion derives from his presentation of the plays through chronological plot summaries – few of his original audience, after all, were acquainted with them – thus obliterating Ibsen's 'retrospective' method and one of his underlying themes, the terrifying power of the past. Other difficulties tend to arise in *The Quintessence* depending on how Ibsen's plays fit Shaw's analytical scheme. Shaw may reasonably describe Brand, for example, as the idealist's image of the perfect man, 'man as it is his duty to be', but it is harder to present the self-indulgent Peer Gynt as the would-be heroic idealist of the 'indomitable will' betrayed by false ideals of love and adventure. Shaw, who thirty years later was to construct his own vast 'world-historical' philosophical drama, not surprisingly spends a good deal of time on *Emperor and Galilean*, even hinting at what he was to call the Life Force, as he attributes the Emperor Julian's failure to his conception of the power opposing him as a rival will and 'not as the whole of which his will was but a part'. Shaw does not spend as much time on *A Doll's House* and *Ghosts*, though these – especially the latter – were the Ibsen plays then agitating London, but focuses sharply on them as attacks on conventional marriage as a bourgeois 'ideal', stressing the rightness of Nora's demand for 'a more honorable relation' to her husband and the hideous consequences of Mrs Alving's having accepted 'the ideal of wifely and womanly duty'. As Shaw proceeds through the plays, he places emphasis where it will best serve his purposes (e.g. in *An Enemy of the People* he focuses on the 'local majority of middle-class people' who 'disguise themselves ideally' as 'The People' or 'Democracy' and largely ignores the ambiguously comic Dr Stockman) and even neglects to deal with material not significant to him (e.g. in *Rosmersholm* he says nothing about Ulric Brendel or Rebecca's sexual past). Nevertheless, despite such apparent high-handedness, *The Quintessence* is full of perceptive comments (e.g. on Nora's sexual teasing of Dr Rank), for there is a profound underlying sympathy between these writers.

That sympathy is evident partly in the more sensitive treatment of the works covered in the chapter 'The Last Four Plays' that Shaw added in 1913 with its gravely eloquent portrait of Ibsen after his stroke 'creeping ghost-like through the blackening mental darkness . . . sitting at a copybook, like a child, trying to learn again how to write, only to find that divine power gone forever from his dead hand'. Moreover, Shaw finds himself sensing an affinity with his own work as he describes the relationship between Rita and Allmers in *Little Eyolf*: 'In short, they form the ideal home of romance; and it would be hard to find a compacter or more effective formula for a small private hell'. The association of romance and hell evokes *Man and Superman*, as does his distinguishing in *When We Dead Awaken* the theme he had postulated in his own play but not developed, that of the artist who wastes 'the modern woman's soul to rouse his imagination'. But there are further affinities. It has been suggested that Shaw's early plays are themselves exercises in 'destroying ideals', and the argument has some validity.[8] A deeper bond stretches even beyond the inversion of the 'doll's house' pattern in *Candida*, where the husband as Shaw himself tells us, is revealed as the coddled 'doll' and where after the discussion scene at the end of the play the poet, who had previously seemed weak, even feminine, leaves, no longer desiring what he now recognises as a debilitating domesticity. It is in the contrast between Morell, who remains in the world to do its necessary socialist work, and Marchbanks, who leaves it for a higher realm of being, that we find the most significant and most deeply submerged equivalence between Shaw and Ibsen. For just as Shaw expressed his own divided impulses (of commitment to the world and rejection of it) by repeating this pattern in his work (Anderson and Dudgeon, Cleopatra and Caesar, Tanner and Don Juan, Charles and Joan are only a few examples), so Ibsen struggling with his vision of self-realisation, expressed it in the contrast between the earthly and the exalted natures that recurs throughout his work: Peer Gynt and Brand, Hjalmar and Gregers, Rebecca and Rosmer; the list could continue. Shaw's imaginative reach towards Ibsen may well have exceeded his intellectual grasp, but he nevertheless seized upon an unresolved conflict at the heart of Ibsen's drama, recreated it in Shavian terms, and placed it – still unresolved – at the heart of his own.

When, five years after the Ibsen lecture to the Fabian Society, Shaw became drama critic of *The Saturday Review*, he remained a committed Ibsenite, attempting on occasion to bully the leader of the British stage, Sir Henry Irving, into performing Ibsen, as well as Shaw's own plays, and keeping a vigilant eye on such Ibsen productions as were accessible. Even with his admired Mrs Patrick Campbell, for whom he was to create the role of Eliza Doolittle, he was ruthless when in December of 1896 she took over the part of Rita Allmers in *Little Eyolf* from the Ibsen actress Janet Achurch and, in Shaw's view, altered the tone of the performance disastrously. 'Mrs Campbell succeeded wonderfully', he wrote with acidulous irony, 'in eliminating all unpleasantness from the play.... Goodness gracious, I thought, what things that evil-minded Miss Achurch did read into this harmless play! And how nicely Mrs Campbell took the drowning of the child! Just a pretty waving of the fingers, a moderate scream as if she had very nearly walked on a tin tack, and it was all over, without tears, without pain, without more fuss than if she had broken the glass of her watch.'

Shaw could sound the Ibsenite note of moral independence even when discussing the work of other playwrights. In his first review he commented on Oscar Wilde's recently opened *An Ideal Husband*, claiming that one of the characters had asserted the courage of his crime 'as against the mechanical idealism of his stupidly good wife'. Not only does the phrase describe Wilde's Lady Chiltern but it evokes the incongruous presence of Mrs Alving, Ibsen's tragic exemplar of 'mechanical idealism' in a wife guiltily clutching the box of morphia tablets. Even when reviewing a play by Henry Arthur Jones, whom Shaw seems most to have admired among contemporary British dramatists, he judges by firmly Ibsenite standards, complaining that because the central figure of *Michael and His Lost Angel* publicly admits guilt for a sexual indiscretion even though he cannot regret his love affair, he forfeits any claim to being a hero. 'Let me rewrite the last three acts', Shaw demands, 'and you shall have your Reverend Michael embracing the answer of his own soul, thundering it from the steps of the altar, and marching out through his shocked and shamed parishioners, with colors flying and head erect and unashamed, to the freedom of faith in his own real conscience.' Shaw stops just short of suggesting that Michael brandish a copy of *A Doll's House* under the noses of the churchwardens.

It was not only the ponderous technique of Arthur Wing Pinero, his other widely admired contemporary, of which Shaw complained, but his failure to achieve even Jones' degree of intellectual consistency. In February of 1895 Shaw commented on the recently published *The Second Mrs Tanqueray*, which had established Pinero as, supposedly, the leading intellectual playwright of the day, noting with mischievous precision its technical inadequacies ('the hero at his own dinner party is compelled to get up and go ignominiously into the next room to write some letters when something has to be said behind his back') but focusing on Pinero's lack 'of the higher dramatic gift of sympathy with character' and his tendency to judge from his own point of view 'in terms of the conventional systems of morals'. When the heroine sentimentalises with her husband about her innocent girlhood, Shaw explodes with an Ibsenite's annoyance:

> One can imagine how, in a play by a master-hand, Paula's reply would have opened Tanqueray's foolish eyes to the fact that a woman of that sort is already the same at three as she is at thirty-three, and that however she may have found by experience that her nature is in conflict with the ideals of differently constituted people, she remains perfectly valid to herself, and despises herself, if she sincerely does so at all, for the hypocrisy that the world forces on her instead of for being what she is.

Shaw could hardly be less than contemptuous of Pinero for having, as he said in reviewing *The Notorious Mrs Ebbsmith* a few weeks later, 'no idea beyond that of doing something daring and bringing down the house by running away from the consequences', for in the previous year Shaw had written *Mrs Warren's Profession*, in which he had distinguished more finely even than this didactic passage suggests how a 'fallen' woman is herself from the first, as well as the way she accepts the 'ideals' of society and is, as her daughter calls her, 'a conventional woman after all'.

But inevitably Shaw as a reviewer usually had to concern himself with performances of plays far more ephemeral even than those of Jones and Pinero. He reveals in these notices an engagement with the art of acting almost as profound as his commitments to politics and drama. His discrimination of the brilliantly calculated theatricality of Bernhardt from the genuinely emotive effects of Duse is an object lesson in precise theatrical observation and a clue to his ability to produce both rich characterisations and remarkable acting parts. Particularly striking moments occur in his review, in June of 1895, of Sardou's *Fedora* entitled 'sardoodledom' (Shaw coined the term to ridicule the mechanical emptiness of the well-made play). Here he anticipates his later personal infatuation with Mrs Patrick Campbell, who played the lead: 'It was not Fedora; but it was Circe'. Nevertheless, Shaw went on to try to resist her blandishments, 'to be Ulysses', as he said, and to be Pygmalion – that is, to be the elocution teacher of his later play – and explain that because Mrs Pat articulated 'with the tip of her tongue against her front teeth as much as possible', her diction was 'technically defective'. Intriguingly, Shaw's own dramatic style reflects his deep absorption, not only with Ibsen and the other contemporary masters, but with the activity of that commercial theatre against which he battled with such whimsical passion.

Despite the persistence with which Shaw inveighed against the vapidity of most of the plays presented to him for review, it was to these plays – to the standard dramatic types of the London stage as it then was, and indeed to those of the Dublin theatre as it had been in his boyhood – that he turned for material he could transform into his uniquely Shavian creations. For this purpose the great drama of Ibsen that he so much admired was hardly sufficiently malleable. Ibsen's retrospective method of gradual revelation reflected his sense of the inescapable power of one's past life over the present. But Shaw's vision was, consciously at least, turned to the future, to a new society and even a new species. One type of Shavian drama, the Discussion Play, may derive from Ibsen, whose special technical contribution, Shaw had said, was the discussion of significant issues as part of the play. But by

1913, when Shaw made this assertion, claiming that some of his own plays had expanded on Ibsen's innovation, he had already written such discursive works as *Getting Married* and *Misalliance*, and he may well have been justifying his own practice after the fact. Certainly the brooding concentration of Ibsen's work, always spiralling downward toward some terrifying discovery, seems to have little to do with the playful freedom of Shaw's dramatic disquisitions, which so often work by accretion, adding jokes, new characters, even new themes as the work progresses. But the conventional theatrical mechanisms of the age gave him exactly the freedom he needed. Because they were not inextricably bound to a significant vision of life, they were, in effect, largely empty, and Shaw could fill them with his own substance, make of them whatever he liked. Or if they had any content, it was of an entirely conventional sort; when Shaw altered it, the new thought was the more delightfully incongruous in the old context. Moreover, these plays offered him a further gift in the form of the simple theatrical pleasures – of suspense, excitement, amusement – that Shaw rarely disdained. It was not merely that Shaw wanted his plays to be successful, although he did, or that he was sugar-coating his intellectual pill, although he was, but that by making his work entertaining in quite ordinary ways, he satisfied a genuinely personal need. The Puritan instinct that led Shaw the artist and philosopher to be also a vestryman and socialist orator demanded, paradoxically, that he entertain as well as instruct. It bound him to do the work to which he had laid his hand, in this case the everyday work of the theatrical world.

Even as he did this work, however, he transformed it into the higher labour of his art. Seizing upon the familiar genres of the stage as he knew it, Shaw kept many of their primary theatrical virtues while giving them an intellectual density, and indeed an emotional force, that took them far from their origins. Thus the familiar courtesan or 'fallen woman' play such as *The Lady of the Camellias* or *The Second Mrs Tanqueray* became in his hands not a perfumed tragedy or a romance of redemption through love but, in *Mrs Warren's Profession*, a dramatised study, in part at least, of the economics of prostitution with a busy, self-satisfied madam in place of the usual repentant magdalen. Many of the standard ingredients of a nineteenth-century melodrama – a last-minute rescue, a noble sacrifice, even a hero who is kind to an orphan-child – remain intact in *The Devil's Disciple,* but the sacrifice is not made for love, much to the shock and distress of the heroine, but out of an asexual religious instinct, and the 'heavy' villain turns out to be an amiable proto-Superman who gets along splendidly with the hero. The traditional romantic comedy with the Cinderella motif recurs in *Pygmalion*, but here, after Cinderella passes the test at the ball and demonstrates her true nobility, it turns out that the Prince is too much interested in his profession and his mother to care very much whether or not she continues to live in his castle.[9] Shaw's plays are usually related to general types; occasionally, however, a specific analogue can be observed, and there the comparison is especially apt.

In May of 1895 Shaw began writing a one-act play on Napoleon, and he was still working on it that July when he saw the French actress Réjane in Sardou's Napoleon play, *Madame Sans-Gêne*. Although he missed some of it because of his limited command of spoken French, he did not hesitate to describe it (correctly) in his review as having 'twenty minutes or so of amusement' and as being 'a huge mock historic melodrama which never for a moment produces the faintest conviction'. Nevertheless, there are

similarities between it and his own play: in both, Napoleon
flirts with and loses his temper with a clever woman who is
trying to protect a secret of his wife's, and in both he
intrigues for and intercepts a letter concerning her fidelity.
But the differences are more significant than the
likenesses. In his review (April 1897) of the English
production starring Ellen Terry and Henry Irving, Shaw
wrote that Sardou's Napoleon 'is nothing but the jealous
husband of a thousand fashionable dramas, talking
Buonapartiana'. This is not quite fair, for Shaw's
Napoleon spouts a certain amount of Buonapartiana
himself: 'And have you no devouring devil inside you who
must be fed with action and victory: gorged with them
night and day . . . who is at once your slave and your
tyrant, your genius and your doom. . . ?' But Shaw is
right about the jealous husband: Sardou's Napoleon rages
about his doubts in an utterly commonplace manner:
'Tous les soupçons, et, grâce à vous, misérables femmes,
pas une certitude!' [Every suspicion, and, thanks to you,
wretched women, not one certainty].[10] Had they been
confirmed, he would clearly have behaved exactly like
Torvald Helmer. In contrast, Shaw's Napoleon makes use
of 'ideal' attitudes, of noble generosity and self-denial, as
mere stratagems, but when he finally reads the letter
attesting to Josephine's guilt, he is unashamedly beyond
any scruples in contriving to ignore it. Shaw not only
manages the familiar intrigue with vastly more wit and
adroitness than Sardou, but at its climax he alters the
standard attitudes to offer a flash of original moral
perception. And whereas Sardou pads his thin material
with whole scenes of tedious irrelevance, to be carried off
by the mere charm of the leading actress, Shaw keeps his
plot tight but allows himself as a climax, a grandly
expansive, aria-like discourse by Napoleon offering an

occasion for the highest elocutionary virtuosity by the actor.

Shaw was able to manipulate the materials of the traditional theatre not only because he was a close and penetrating observer of it but because, as his career progressed, he became a skilled and active practitioner. Shaw was often the producer – in American terminology, director – of his own plays, and quickly became a thoroughly competent, efficient theatre person, deeply involved in details of casting, design, and rehearsal. In an age when plays were usually staged by an actor-manager primarily concerned with making an effect in his own part, Shaw maintained that producing was a separate task ('You cannot conduct an orchestra and play the drum at the same concert') and that the author was best qualified to perform it. Meticulous in rehearsal preparation, he carefully blocked movements ahead of time to 'set' the actors for their big speeches and get them quickly off when they were finished. Above all, Shaw was a brilliant handler of actors – his own lifelong performance in the role of G. B. S. no doubt sensitising him to their needs – recognising which ones could be trusted to find their own way in a role and which required detailed coaching. He was capable, for example, of writing whole paragraphs to Lillah McCarthy (the original Anne Whitefield) on how to get the right effect in a single crucial line of *The Doctor's Dilemma*. Usually he was careful to offer actors advice in private, and even when he bullied, it was with a sweetly comic exuberance, as in this letter of 29 November 1905 to Louis Calvert, the original Undershaft of *Major Barbara*, who had not learned his lines: 'I have taken a box for Friday and had a hundredweight of cabbages, dead cats, eggs, and gingerbeer bottles stacked in it. Every word you fluff, every speech you unact, I will shy something at you. . . . You are an impostor, a sluggard, a blockhead, a shirk, a malingerer, and the worst actor that ever lived or ever will live. I will apologize to the public for engaging you: I will tell your mother of you'.

Shaw worked hard to achieve a large, rhetorical, 'operatic' delivery for his own plays, something that would go beyond the conventional drawing-room style of the day, but he was not interested in directorial innovation in itself even though he was the contemporary of such figures as Stanislavsky, Reinhardt, and Antoine. He had conceived of his drama in terms of the nineteenth-century theatre, and most of his work as a producer was carried on within its limits. When his plays came to be adapted for the screen, he brought the same skill and shrewdness to his work as a screenwriter, though his age by then prevented him from undertaking direction.[11] The best testimony to Shaw's judgement here is that the successful film versions of his plays were made during his lifetime by the producer of his choice, Gabriel Pascal (*Pygmalion, Major Barbara, Caesar and Cleopatra*) and that later efforts have ranged from indifferent (*The Doctor's Dilemma*) to downright bad (*The Devil's Disciple*).

4
Plays of the Nineties

In July of 1899 Shaw finished *Captain Brassbound's Conversion*, the last of what he was to publish the following January as the *Three Plays for Puritans*. Having written the part of Lady Cicely for Ellen Terry, he sent the play off to her at once, and at the beginning of August while waiting for her reply – initially unfavourable, though six years later she did the role – he wrote to her mentioning his future plans: 'And now no more plays – at least no more practicable ones. None at all, indeed, for some time to come: it is time to do something more in Shaw-philosophy, in politics & sociology. Your author, dear Ellen, must be more than a common dramatist'. Like most of Shaw's letters to Ellen Terry this one has at least three entangled purposes: to carry on his fantasy romance with her, impassioned and yet safely literary; to further his long-term strategy of using the Irving–Terry Lyceum in the interests of the new drama; to further his short-term tactic of having Ellen Terry act in his new play. This comment of Shaw's, however, does more than merely slither between flattery, in suggesting the uncommon status of dear Ellen's author, and threat, in declaring that there will not be any suitable plays from him after this one. It marks Shaw's awareness that he was moving from one stage of his career to another.

In the seven years since Shaw had committed himself to the drama, he had written ten plays. Not all of them had been produced, but he was known and had earned enough in royalties to give up journalism. Moreover, the physical breakdown of the previous year, 1898, that had been a significant factor in his accepting the domestic security of marriage, must have suggested to him that there were limits even to his awesome capacities for work. For whatever combination of reasons, Shaw now paused in his labour as a playwright. Four years passed before he in-augurated the next stage of his career with the completion of a significant new play, this one unlike its predecessors to be published in a volume by itself. *Man and Superman* was no 'practicable' play, its length alone making a complete performance almost impossible in the theatre of its time and rare even today. Shaw now wrote not as a 'common dramatist' but as an artist-philosopher.

His new status, however, did not prevent Shaw from writing plays that were viable in the theatre; even *Man and Superman*, in fact, was presentable in conventional circumstances when separated from its disquisitory Act III. But now he wrote in an assured, characteristic voice, whereas in the earlier plays, though some are among his most attractive and enduring achievements, he had shifted restlessly, brilliantly from genre to genre searching for a mode in which he could appeal to a theatre audience and yet function as an artist. With Ellen Terry's initial rejection of *Captain Brassbound*, Shaw at least claimed to put aside the question of immediate theatrical success:

'No', he wrote to her on 4 August 1899, 'it is clear that I have nothing to do with the theatre of today: I must educate a new generation with my pen from childhood up – audience, actors and all, and leave them my plays to murder after I am cremated.' Happily, the Vedrenne-Barker management at the Court Theatre was shortly to undertake the education of his audience, not a few years prior to his cremation; but, even allowing for Shaw's whimsical striking of attitudes, he had clearly resolved that, whatever the consequences, he would proceed in his own way.

He did so, without substantial interruption, for exactly twenty years. The central creative portion of Shaw's career began with the appearance of *Man and Superman* in 1903 and concluded with that of *Saint Joan* in 1923. Had Shaw been solicitous of the critical taste for symmetry, he might have postponed the publication of *Back to Methuselah* (1921) for two years and thus concluded this chapter of his work as he had begun it with a lengthy dramatised exegesis of his religious ideas. But of course Shaw could hardly have recognised in advance that *Saint Joan* was to represent the last full flowering of his powers. When he returned to the theatre with *The Apple Cart* after a five-year interregnum, he brought with him a different kind of play, a 'political extravaganza' as he called it, and noticeably diminished powers. Nevertheless, the plays of the last period are still Shavian. Whatever their limitations, they are full of wit and charm, and for any other dramatist would have been a distinguished life's work.

Just as these final plays make their own claims on one's attention and offer their own rewards, so do the early works from *Widowers' Houses* through *Brassbound*. None of them is without interest; some are masterpieces. Moreover, it was through these plays that Shaw established the thematic concerns and the patterns of dramatic action through which he was thereafter to project his vision of life. He published them in three groups, following the order of their composition: *Plays Unpleasant, Plays Pleasant,* and *Three Plays for Puritans.* Of these works, the plays in the first are simultaneously the least and the most significant.

'Plays Unpleasant'

They are the least significant for obvious reasons: all of them show a certain awkwardness that Shaw was quickly to overcome. There are stretches of rambling dialogue, some uncertain characterisations, instances of notably clumsy stage-management. Moreover, *Widowers' Houses* and *Mrs Warren's Profession* address immediate economic issues, slum landlordism and the exploitation of female workers as the basis of prostitution, that Shaw, for all his continuing commitment to socialism, never again turned to in the drama. But the very awkwardness and harshness of these 'unpleasant' plays reveal, behind their social concerns, some of the central Shavian obsessions that dominate his work from the first. Motifs that later become richly transformed, and thus to some degree disguised, are here presented openly, even crudely, allowing one to glimpse for a moment things that are hardly to be seen so directly again.

Part of the problem in perceiving Shaw clearly and assessing him justly lies in the division in his own nature and thus in his aims as a writer. One aspect of this conflict appears in the first of Shaw's prefaces, a brief one written for the publication of *Widowers' Houses* in 1893 as the initial volume in the 'Independent Theatre Series'. Most of it is a humorous defence of the liberties he had taken with Archer's mechanically 'well made' libretto of 1885, which had been shortly abandoned when Archer could not keep up with Shaw's demands for more plot and then finished for Grein's Independent Theatre in 1892. Protesting that his play is better than anything turned out by the 'patent constructive machinery' school of drama, Shaw claims that it is 'in intention a work of art as much as any comedy of Molière's is a work of art', and then asserts firmly in the next sentence that its quality is only enhanced 'by the fact that it deals with a burning social question, and is deliberately intended to induce people to vote on the Progressive side at the next County Council election in London'.[1] Shaw took a less assertive stance in the 1898 preface to the *Plays Unpleasant*, granting that on the occasion of the play's production, when he 'at once became infamous as a playwright', it had been presented 'with all its original tomfooleries on its head' and had made an effect 'out of all proportion to its merits or even its demerits'. The later view is certainly the more just, but the earlier catches something of the play's tangled, contradictory quality. For Shaw writes what is at once an elusive, personal work of art about people's emotive lives and an insistent piece of economic propaganda.

In both guises *Widowers' Houses* has a number of obvious demerits, some of an elementary, technical nature. First of all, the entire play is founded on a vast coincidence: that on a continental vacation the youthful hero, Dr Harry Trench, should meet and become desperately infatuated with the daughter of a great slum landlord, Sartorius, who manages, among other properties, the one from which, though he is unaware of its source, his own income derives. Moreover, in Act I a two-and-a-half-page proposal scene, which cannot possibly be stretched to more than a few minutes' playing time, is supposed to allow Blanche's father and Trench's confidant to leave, tour a local church, and return. Later, when Trench and his friend come to his prospective father-in-law's home, Sartorius actually leaves them alone with his agent, whom he has just discharged for disobedience, thus offering an opportunity – golden, but improbable – for Lickcheese, the agent, to reveal the true source of Sartorius' wealth. The return of Lickcheese, abruptly converted from a desperate worm to a successful real estate manipulator in his own right, is, like the confidant's reappearance as his secretary, merely incredible; Shaw treats the same joke more imaginatively in *Pygmalion* with the return of Doolittle, simultaneously elevated and crushed. And finally, once Trench has accepted Sartorius' defence of his business in Act II, there is no dramatic action for Act III except clearing up the misunderstanding with Blanche. When Shaw reworks this material in *Major Barbara,* he is a wiser craftsman; the fiancé's conversion by the 'wicked' father is the climactic struggle, placed with greatest effect at the end of the play.

In his own way Archer was quite correct: Shaw had used up all the plot before the end of Act II. The great social revelations had been made, to everyone except the heroine, and the arguments about them had been held. It is important to be clear about the nature of these revelations: they are not that slums are terrible and that rents are gouged out of the poor, although Shaw cannot resist an impassioned explication of those truths. 'Why, see here gentlemen!' cries Lickcheese, whose Dickensian name prefigures his rhetorical style, 'Look at that bag of money on the table. Hardly a penny of that but there was a hungry child crying for the bread it would have bought'. Nor do they lie in Lickcheese's assertion that his character is the result of social circumstances ('I'm poor: that's enough to make a rascal of me') or even in Sartorius' curiously modern argument about the difficulties of providing adequate housing ('these poor people do not know how to live in proper dwellings: they would wreck them in a week'). Rather the revelations derive from the 'discussion', to use Shaw's Ibsenite term, that follows Trench's conventionally heroic reaction to the discovery that his future father-in-law's money, which was to support the young couple in appropriate style, is tainted.

In the noblest theatrical manner, Trench confronts the ogre, denounces him for having made his money 'out of a parcel of unfortunate creatures that have hardly enough to keep body and soul together . . . by screwing, and bullying, and threatening, and all sorts of pettifogging tyranny', and rejects his ill-gotten wealth. This was the point at which the original play was to have ended. But now, in place of the muttered threats of the conventional melodramatic villain, Trench is greeted by a thoroughly rational explanation of the economics of the real estate business. He is assured that Sartorius is, like himself, 'a sound Conservative', who has worked hard for his money and provided accommodations for the poor at 'the recognized fair London rent'. And finally he learns that his own hands are far from clean, for his income derives from a mortgage on one of Sartorius' properties. His moral assurance shattered, Trench gasps 'Do you mean to say that I am just as bad as you are?' 'If', Sartorius replies, 'you meant that you are just as powerless to alter the state of society, then you are unfortunately quite right!' The Shavian implication, ironically inherent in Sartorius' words, is that if Trench were not a 'sound Conservative' but a socialist, he would not be, as Shaw describes him, '*morally beggared*'.

But Trench's problems have not been economic only. As he has failed in his effort to play the Man of Honour with Sartorius, so a few moments earlier he had failed in an attempt to play the Scrupulous Lover with Blanche. Far too much of a gentleman to explain to his fiancée the source of her father's wealth but, at that point, determined to reject it, he tells her that he is too proud to take money, lest it be thought he had married for it, and hopes that she will settle for romantic love and modest comfort instead of luxury. Blanche, however, declines the role of the clinging, devoted heroine. Not only does she want the money for itself, but she wants to be independent of her husband. When Trench persists, she assumes he is attempting to escape the engagement, flies into a rage, and breaks it off. Trench, who has been proceeding on the traditionally 'idealistic' view – traditional, that is, in the theatre – that love conquers all, finds that it does nothing of the sort. Ultimately, when the money matters have been arranged, Blanche and Tench are united, but it is not so much love that conquers as what Shaw would call, with characteristic fastidiousness, concupiscence. The progress of sexuality through this play is at least as significant as the progress of economics.

It begins with the proposal scene of Act I, which is founded on traditional comic materials: a shy and awkward young man being led on by a determined girl. It even climaxes in the same joke Wilde uses in the proposal scene of *The Importance of Being Earnest*. Labouring under the delusion that because he has kissed Blanche he has proposed to her, Trench forces her to exclaim – like Gwendolen rebuking Jack – 'But you havnt said anything'. Yet quite unlike Gwendolen, a creation of Wilde's most elegant fantasy, Blanche, a creation of Shaw's doubts and fears, is both sensual and crudely calculating. Shaw's stage directions are more revelatory than the characters' speeches:

> TRENCH: [*alarmed*] I say: youre not offended, are you? [*She looks at him for a moment with a reproachful film on her eyes*]. Blanche. [*She bristles instantly; overdoes it; and frightens him*]. I beg your pardon for calling you by your name; but I – er – [*She corrects her mistake by softening her expression eloquently. He responds with a gush*] You dont mind, do you? I felt sure you wouldnt, somehow. Well, look here. . . . [*he flounders more and more, unable to see that she can hardly contain her eagerness*].

When Shaw rewrites the scene of the awkward young man and the designing girl in *Man and Superman*, he has a philosophic justification for the woman's social and sexual demands, so Ann Whitefield can be allowed a genuine grace and charm that are denied to Blanche.

However, in a scene near the end of the second act of *Widowers' Houses* Shaw let slip the most fearful image of feminine sexuality that he was to permit himself in the whole of his career. Though brief, it is startling both for its content and what seems to be its irrelevance. Having broken with Trench, Blanche is furiously wrapping up his letter and gifts; she asks a devoted and submissive parlourmaid why she is crying:

> PARLORMAID: [*plaintively*] You speak so brutal to me, Miss Blanche; and I do love you so. I'm sure no one else would stay and put up with what I have to put up with.
>
> BLANCHE: Then go. I dont want you. Do you hear. Go.

PARLORMAID: [*piteously, falling on her knees*] Oh no, Miss Blanche. Dont send me away from you: dont –
BLANCHE: [*with fierce disgust*] Agh! I hate the sight of you. [*The maid, wounded to heart, cries bitterly*]. Hold your tongue. Are those two gentlemen gone?
PARLORMAID: [*weeping*] Oh, how could you say such a thing to me, Miss Blanche: me that –
BLANCHE: [*seizing her by the hair and throat*] Stop that noise, I tell you, unless you want me to kill you.
PARLORMAID: [*protesting and imploring, but in a carefully subdued voice*] Let me go, Miss Blanche: you know youll be sorry: you always are. Remember how dreadfully my head was cut last time.

The suggestion that Blanche and her maid have a long-standing sado-masochistic relationship with overtones of barely repressed lesbianism makes this scene a curious, quasi-pornographic intrusion on a play that has seemed to be concerned with quite other matters. Extraordinary as this episode is, a moment later it is nearly surpassed in passionate intensity by a scene in which Blanche's emotional interest is focused on yet another figure, her father. Although Sartorius tells her that the difficulty with Trench has been got over, Blanche disregards his words and begs his permission to do as she wishes in regard to the marriage. Abruptly the self-controlled businessman becomes an indulgent, even infatuated parent:

SARTORIUS: [*abandoning his self-control, and giving way recklessly to his affection for her*] You shall do as you like now and always, my beloved child. I only wish to do as my own darling pleases.
BLANCHE: Then I will not marry him. He has played fast and loose with me. He thinks us beneath him: he

is ashamed of us: he dared to object to being benefited by you – as if it were not natural for him to owe you everything; and yet the money tempted him after all. [*She throws her arms hysterically about his neck*] Papa: I dont want to marry: I only want to stay with you and be happy as we have always been. I hate the thought of being married: I dont care for him: I dont want to leave you. [*Trench and Cokane come in; but she can hear nothing but her own voice and does not notice them*]. Only send him away: promise me that you will send him away and keep me here with you as we have always – [*seeing Trench*] Oh! [*She hides her face on her father's breast*].

Both of these scenes are far more intense than anything required by the plot, which demands only that the reunion of Blanche and her fiancé be postponed to the third act. Clearly they are psychological fantasies concerning child-parent relationships: one rooted in fear, the other in wish-fulfilment. In the first scene the domineering, authoritarian figure (the mistress *in loco parentis*) takes pleasure in being cruel as the submissive, childlike partner, though gratified by the contact, is punished for desiring affection. (The cruelty here is in a curious way legitimised by the fantasy: the forbidden lesbianic love of the maid for the mistress may be seen as deserving the punishment that would not be appropriate to a child making impassioned demands on the affections of a parent.) In the second scene the authoritarian woman, though still assertive in rejecting her lover, now assumes the child's role and reverts to a dream of endless incestuous bliss, which desire the loving parent gratifies. In this tangle of erotic impulses, never again to be expressed so openly, Shaw prefigures the conflicting fears and wishes that were to haunt his characters throughout his career as a playwright. Parental figures tend to evoke highly ambiguous attitudes in the world of the Shavian drama, sometimes fiercely rejected like Kitty Warren, sometimes idealised like Andrew Undershaft. The conception of Blanche as mistress/ mother, stern but beloved, is particularly significant, for in Shaw the erotic is rarely entirely separate from the maternal, nor the maternal from some hint of cruelty. Inevitably the neuroses of any artist will colour his vision while at the same time offering him insights denied to one who has not travelled through the same psychic countryside. The very limitations imposed on Shaw's affections in childhood seem to have left him as an artist, with a rich sense of the complex attractions and repulsions of eroticism, especially as manifested in familial relations.

Certainly, these conflicting emotions go far to explain the oddities of Act III of *Widowers' Houses*. In Act II, in his conversation with Sartorius, the well-meaning Trench had only been persuaded to recognise what was in Shaw's view the inescapable moral dilemma posed by unearned income. Now, however, he quickly joins in a shabby plan to defraud the municipal authorities. But what seems an inconsistency in characterisation is, in a deeper mode, emotively in tune with the ending of the play. For Trench is drawn not only into a world of economic corruption but into one of squalid physicality as well. Again it is the stage directions that reveal the nature of this 'fallen' world as Blanche and Trench meet again: '*For a moment they stand face to face, quite close to one another, she provocative, taunting, half defying, half inviting him to advance, in a flush of undisguised animal excitement. It suddenly flashes on him that all this ferocity is erotic: that she is making love to him*'. Looking at her with his eyes '*full of delight*', Trench responds to her erotic power: '*She flings her arms around him, and crushes him in an ecstatic embrace'*. The 'greater damnation' promised to those 'which devour widows' houses' is for Shaw undoubtedly the social condemnation so fiercely implied in his ironic twisting of the biblical phrase.[2] But there is another, less obvious kind of damnation for Shaw: it is to be condemned, like Trench (who does indeed sink into a kind of abyss), to the fleshly world of common life. The greater Shavian heroes make their peace with this world in various ways, but none is entirely free of the desire to escape its demands.

One of the processes of escape is delineated in Shaw's next play *The Philanderer*. Written in 1893, it was not performed professionally till 1907, though Shaw had suggested it to both Richard Mansfield and Ellen Terry. The latter must have thought his recommendation rather odd since, after rereading it, he had already described it to her in a letter of August 1896 as 'a combination of mechancial farce with realistic filth which quite disgusted me'. In fact the play is lively, rambling but very stageable, full of good-natured satire rather than mechanical farce, and has so little of 'realistic filth' that in it Shaw has desexualised the circumstances on which its first scene is based, the occasion on which Jenny Patterson, the long-time mistress from whom he was trying to disentangle himself, interrupted an assignation between him and Florence Farr: 'In the evening I went to F.E. [Emery was Florence Farr's married name]; and JP burst in on us very late in the evening. There was a most shocking scene; JP being violent and using atrocious language. At last I sent F.E. out of the room, having to restrain J.P. by force from attacking her. I was two hours getting her out of the house . . .'.[3] Nothing in the play suggests that the relations between the 'Ibsenist philosopher' Charteris, the *'beautiful, dark, tragic looking'* Julia Craven, a distinctly younger, glamourised version of Jenny Patterson, and Grace Tranfield have gone beyond flirting, kissing, and a sincere proposal of marriage from Charteris to Grace. The squalid scene that in reality ended only at 3:00 a.m. when Shaw was able to get free of Mrs Patterson explodes on stage into comic alarums and confusions when the fathers of the two women unexpectedly arrive.

Ultimately, everything is tended to in humorous terms. A husband is found for Julia in the infatuated, appropriately named Dr Paramore, whose ludicrous medical obsession prefigures those of certain of the physicians in *The Doctor's Dilemma*. The emotional reality of Julia's '*keen sorrow*' appears only in the final stage direction, but meanwhile she has, in a moment of anger, revealed the same mixture of the maternal and the sexually domineering seen in Blanche at the end of *Widowers' Houses*

> JULIA: You fraud! You humbug! You miserable little plaster saint! . . . Oh [*In a paroxysm half of rage, half of tenderness, she shakes him, growling over him like a tigress over a cub*].

Shaw is not yet able to dignify feminine animality, as he does in *Man and Superman* by seeing it as an aspect of the Life Force, but he does offer a rationale for the obsessive interest of the 'Ibsenist philosopher' in women when Julia describes him as more of a vivisector than the doctor: 'Yes; but then I learn so much more from my experiments than he does!' This is a version of the artist's ruthless examination of women spoken of by Don Juan. Finally Charteris is rescued from marriage by even more dubious arguments when Grace rejects him by claiming in Act II that, since she loves him too much, he would have a 'terrible advantage' over her if they married, and in Act III that, since Charteris has learned how to treat women from Julia and her like and therefore cannot give love and respect, she will choose respect. These are not quite the same reasons, but they serve the same purpose, to release the Shavian hero from the emotional and physical demands of the common world.

Having successfully dramatised a comic escape from the world rather than a tragic capture by it, Shaw returns in his next work to his initial play, producing a striking thematic variation on it which, if not quite a masterpiece, is the first Shavian play to hold a viable place in the modern repertory. But to disguise its repetitions, no doubt from himself, he made certain radical alterations: the 'wicked' parent is now changed from a father to a mother; the unsavoury source of the family's wealth which has been concealed from the child is not slum landlordism but prostitution; and the young person who discovers that the sustaining money has been tainted is not the daughter's fiancé but the daughter herself. And like its predecessor *Mrs Warren's Profession* is problematic in more than one way.

The theme of prostitution and the hint of incest at the end of Act III made the play almost unstageable in the 1890s; even the hardy J. T. Grein of the Independent Theatre did not like it. There were two private performances in 1902, but it was not till the mid-twenties that the Lord Chamberlain's ban was lifted and the play performed publicly in England. But more important now is a central structural problem: like *Widowers' House, Mrs Warren* seems to be, from one point of view at least, finished by the end of Act II. Here in a scene carefully prepared beforehand when hints about the dubiety of Mrs Warren's background are carefully dropped, Vivie confronts her mother and finds that the money that paid for her comfortable upbringing, her expensive education, and in effect her position in society has come from her mother's occupations, first as a prostitute and later as a successful and efficient brothelkeeper. This scene is the best that Shaw had written up to then and remains one of his notable achievements for a number of reasons. It has psychological, economic, and theatrical resonances.

The 'fallen' woman was a theatrical staple by the time Shaw wrote *Mrs Warren's Profession*, but the magdalens of the nineteenth-century drama bore little resemblance to Kitty Warren. She is a thoroughly convincing portrait of a woman with little sensibility and plenty of character: practical and hard-headed in her business, peevish and possessive with her daughter, sensual but realistic with the daughter's young man, proud of her success but commonplace in mind, vulgar but easy-going enough: 'a good sort', as the young man says, 'but a bad lot'. By contrast the familiar theatrical figure was beauteous, exquisitely gowned, and generally repentant. She might, like the Lady of the Camellias, be a sentimentalised victim, but even if she was a survivor, she tended to regret her choices. At almost exactly the time that Shaw wrote *Mrs Warren*, Oscar Wilde produced *Lady Windermere's Fan*, which also hinges on a confrontation between a virtuous daughter and sexually erring mother. Mrs Erlynne warns her daughter against following in her footsteps: 'You don't know what it is to fall into the pit, to be despised, mocked abandoned, sneered at – to be an outcast! . . . One pays for one's sin, and then one pays again, and all one's life one pays. You must never know that'. When Vivie asks if her mother would not prefer to have her endure poverty rather than take to the streets, Mrs Warren's reply is in a somewhat different vein: '[*indignantly*] Of course not.

What sort of mother do you take me for! How could you keep your self-respect in such starvation and slavery?' Shaw's perfectly inverted cliché and his oratorical query are as dialogue no more realistic than Wilde's dreadful rhetoric, but they mark a theatrical revolution in the attitude to their subject.

Even the familiar striving of the courtesan to re-enter society Shaw handles freshly. Mrs Warren's sister has achieved it quite easily, and now, in her retirement, chaperones genteel girls in a cathedral town. Mrs Warren, who is bored by society, transfers the desire for an elegant life to her daughter, only to find, to her considerable annoyance, that Vivie is as bored by it as she. But Shaw's denigration of traditional attitudes extends much further. Mrs Warren has not, like Mrs Erlynne, been led astray by youthful passion; indeed, by her lights she has not been led astray at all, except by those who preached traditional virtue to a girl who could not afford it. For Shaw the heart of the matter is not sentiment but money.

When the confrontation in Act II between Vivie and her mother rises to its climax, Mrs Warren gives up the emotional bullying with which she had begun and attacks Vivie with economic facts. Even the writing reflects the shift, for Shaw had lapsed into melodramatic excess when Mrs Warren protested her maternal status: '[*distracted, throwing herself on her knees*] Oh no, no. Stop, stop. I am your mother: I swear it'. But he gives her a fiercely efficient dramatic rhetoric (and even an instinctive grasp of the labour theory of value) as she thrusts home to Vivie the argument that a life of drudgery, danger (from factory conditions) and utter poverty was the only alternative to the one that she and her sister accepted: 'Do you think we were such fools as to let other people trade in our good looks by employing us as shopgirls, or barmaids, or

93

waitresses, when we could trade in them ourselves and get all the profits instead of starvation wages? Not likely'. As Mrs Warren goes on to exalt the virtues of hard work, self-restraint, and sound management that have brought her to her present eminence, Shaw slips into her language mischievously ironic inversions of commonplace moralism. Thus, Mrs Warren expresses her contempt for women who do not save and calculate: 'they've no character; and if there's a thing I hate in a woman, it's want of character'. In explaining the drawbacks of her occupation she neatly reverses the vulgar view of its attractions: 'It's not work that any woman would do for pleasure, goodness knows'. And finally she lists the requirements for success in terms of the sternest puritanism, observing that her line of work is 'worth while to a poor girl, if she can resist temptation' and that such a girl must be not only pretty but 'well conducted and sensible'.

The effect of this playful attack on bourgeois language is to call into serious question the ethics of bourgeois society. The point is not that Mrs Warren is innocent but that a capitalist system that exploits female labour, and by extension the labouring classes generally, is guilty. So intent is Shaw on making his idea clear that during a sharply realistic exchange with Vivie he allows Mrs Warren an oratorical moment somewhat in the Hyde Park style. After asserting that for a young woman without money or special talents prostitution is 'far better than any other employment open to her', she adds, 'I always thought that oughtnt to be. It cant be right, Vivie, that there shoudnt be better opportunities for women'. Shaw's presentation of the wider economic view carries the play into Act III, and here his touch is sure. When Sir George Crofts is stung by Vivie's assertion that he is 'a pretty common sort of scoundrel' for investing capital in Mrs Warren's business,

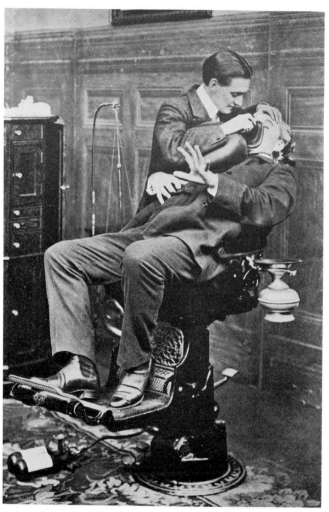

1. *You Never Can Tell*, Royal Court Theatre, 1906: Henry Ainley and Edmund Gurney in Shaw's first public success

2. *Major Barbara*, Royal Court Theatre, 1905: Louis Calvert and Granville Barker

3. *Caesar and Cleopatra*, Savoy Theatre, 1907: Forbes Robertson and Gertrude Elliott

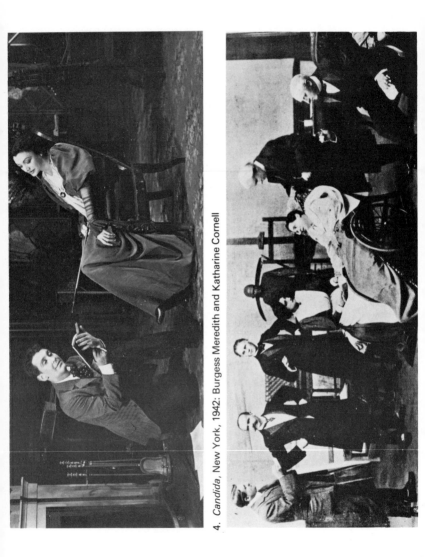

4. *Candida*, New York, 1942: Burgess Meredith and Katharine Cornell

6. *Saint Joan*, New Theatre, 1924: Sybil Thorndike. The production ran for 244 performances

7. *Man and Superman*, New York, 1947: Maurice Evans and Jack Manning

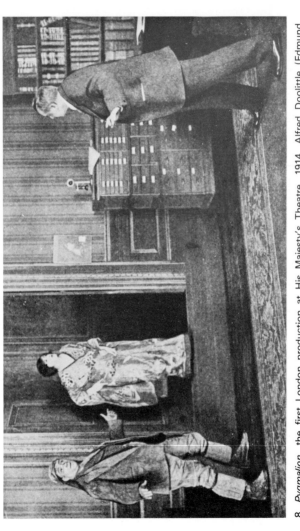

8. *Pygmalion*, the first London production at His Majesty's Theatre, 1914. Alfred Doolittle (Edmund Gurney), Eliza Doolittle (Mrs Patrick Campbell), Henry Higgins (Herbert Tree)

9. *Pygmalion*, New York, 1945: Gertrude Lawrence and Raymond Massey

10. *The Apple Cart*, Malvern Festival, 1929. Sets designed by Paul Shelving

he defends himself with brutal shrewdness, pointing out that the rest of his society does as he does, giving as an example his brother, who has established a scholarship at Vivie's college but whose factory does not pay its women workers enough to live on. 'How d'ye suppose they manage when they have no family to fall back on?' he demands of Vivie. 'Ask your mother'. Having earlier pointed out that Vivie had always been 'in' his and her mother's 'business' since it had supported her, he now argues that all of (capitalist) society is in it as well: 'If youre going to pick and choose your acquaintances on moral principles, youd better clear out of this country, unless you want to cut yourself out of all decent society'.

But what are alternatives for Crofts become for Vivie a double imperative. She cuts herself off from what Crofts supposes to be decent society and, in a sense that he would hardly understand, clears out of the country, obviating thereby the choosing of acquaintances on any principles. While denouncing Crofts as a 'capitalist bully', Vivie is accorded by Shaw an unlikely moment of social, as opposed to moral, consciousness: 'When I think of the society that tolerates you, and the laws that protect you!' If Vivie's career as an actuarial statistician is taken literally, it involves an acceptance of capitalist activity hardly consistent with this denunciation. Indeed, her choice would be little more admirable than Harry Trench's willing acceptance of sharp practices in real estate operation. However, the firm of Fraser and Warren is no more to be taken as merely an accounting business than that of Undershaft and Lazarus is to be understood as merely, or at least exclusively, a munitions manufactory. Rather, the secluded offices of the first and the 'heavenly' city of the second are places where certain Shavian heroes may take refuge from the intolerable circumstances, emotional as well as economic, of the ordinary world.

The psychic lures placed before Vivie are not quite the equal to the maelstrom of sensuality into which Harry Trench is drawn, but they have their own force, and Vivie's resistance to them is the major subject of the last part of her play. They are embodied most notably in the person of Frank Gardner, '*pleasant, pretty, smartly dressed, cleverly good-for-nothing*', as Shaw depicts him in an introductory stage direction, which specifies also that Frank is two years younger than Vivie. The relations between them are difficult to accept – or even to grasp. Frank says that Vivie loves him but, though some very mild sexual play seems to have taken place between them, nothing in Vivie's attitude ever suggests that Frank's claim is justified. As soon as there is serious business at hand, Vivie responds to Frank's advances by pushing him away and telling him that she 'is not in a humor for petting her little boy this evening'. This phrase, coupled with Frank's age, suggests a maternal relationship entangled with the amatory one, just as the effeminising adjective 'pretty' that is applied to Frank, along with Vivie's taste for whisky and cigars, hints at gender reversal. Over and above these dubieties are Frank's more commonplace disadvantages: he is a flirt and has no occupation aside from gambling. As if all this were not sufficient to remove Frank from serious contention as a lover, Shaw adds, in an improbably melodramatic climax to Act III, the information that he may be Vivie's half-brother. (Sir George Crofts, who makes this revelation in a fit of jealous rage after having his own marriage proposal rejected by Vivie, also provides a passing suggestion of incest, since he had for a time entertained the notion that he might be Vivie's father.) Shaw, however, has no interest in writing a Byronic drama

of frustrated passion between brother and sister. Early in
the last act Vivie and Frank assure each other that they
neither believe Crofts' contention nor consider it
significant should it be true.

Nevertheless, the play has made it clear enough why
Vivie should not marry Frank; what it leaves obscure is
why she should not marry someone else, why she should
resolve so firmly to remain 'permanently single'. For Vivie
refuses more than the demands of romantic love; she is no
less adamant in rejecting those of filial duty. The play ends
with a second confrontation between mother and
daughter, hardly less powerful than the first but a great
deal less logical. Shaw portrays Vivie, otherwise strong-
minded, as so shocked at learning from Crofts that her
mother is still practising her profession as to feel that there
can be no further contact between them. In the course of
this tangled argument, in which Vivie rejects the
conventional luxuries Mrs Warren offers, Vivie herself
leads her mother to the irrefutable argument that she
cannot give up brothel keeping because, by temperament,
she must have work and this is the only work she is fit for.
Vivie quite agrees that they are like each other but says:
'my work is not your work, and my way not your way'.
Whatever she may mean by this cryptic remark Vivie does
not pursue her point but goes quickly on to claim that Mrs
Warren has asked her to give up 'the peace and quietness'
of her whole life. Since Mrs Warren plans to continue
living in Brussels and Vienna, it is also hard to know what
Vivie is really saying here, but in any case it is not her final
reason for rejecting her mother, which is that Mrs Warren
has 'lived one life and believed in another' and is therefore
'a conventional woman at heart'. As a rhetorical climax to
their debate, these phrases are sufficiently striking,
especially as Mrs Warren accedes to the notion that Vivie is

right to 'get rid of' her, but it is doubtful that they are an accurate judgement and even more doubtful that they constitute a justification for total separation. What does ring true in their combat is Mrs Warren's fearful claim: 'I want my daughter. Ive a right to you. Who is to care for me when I'm old? . . . Youve no right to turn on me now and refuse to do your duty as a daughter'. And no less absolute is Vivie's total rejection: 'Now once for all, mother, you want a daughter and Frank wants a wife. I dont want a mother; and I dont want a husband'. If this attitude is not explained by Vivie's circumstances in the play, it is to some extent illumined by remembering her creator's circumstances in his childhood. The demanding child and rejecting mother here change places, reversal being one of the simplest of psychic disguises, and the scene reveals itself as a fantasy of revenge that belies Shaw's reputation as a dramatist of ideas who had little access to emotions.

Nor are its economic arguments and psychic underpinnings the only elements out of which the play is made. Praed, the genteel architect, is an unlikely friend for Mrs Warren, but Shaw skates past this improbability to have someone in the play who can suggest to Vivie that she 'saturate' herself 'with beauty and romance' and receive her rejection of these values. Even the Reverend Samuel Gardner, ponderous, fatuous – the *senex* of classical comedy updated to a late-Victorian country clergyman – is more than a creature of the plot. Although he is seen in a humorous rather than a satirical light, he remains a fool. The world that Vivie finally rejects is one in which aesthetics are irrelevant, economics are corrupt, and emotional demands intolerable. And as Shaw's art develops in his next group of plays, it becomes to a greater degree what the characterisation of the Reverend Gardner has suggested, a world of clowns.

'Plays Pleasant'

The brighter coloration of the *Pleasant Plays* (usually so called) is no doubt due in part to Shaw's continuing quest for the theatrical success that had so far eluded him. In the Preface he boasted that he had purposely contrived *Candida* to make its production inexpensive, that *The Man of Destiny* was a 'bravura' acting piece, and that he had cast *You Never Can Tell*, along with his other plays, 'in the ordinary practical comedy form in use at all the theatres'. Though Shaw had no objections to sugar-coating his intellectual pills, some of his claims here derive from his characteristic attitudinising as the man of practicality and efficiency. His very difficulties in achieving successful productions suggest that he had in fact, whatever his intentions, shaped his plays less to the requirements of the commercial stage than to those of his personal vision. For that vision humour is essential. The darker elements, both social and psychological, that dominate the *Unpleasant Plays* remain always as part of Shaw's work, but they are counterbalanced by a vital sense of life and an affectionate view of character. Moreover, humour is absolutely necessary if he is to forward the claims of 'natural morality' to be founded on a 'genuinely scientific natural history' (presumably his own, not yet made publicly explicit) by ridiculing the 'ideals suggested to our imaginations by our half satisfied passions'.

The particular ideal that *Arms and the Man* set out to denigrate was the romantic dream of military glory. So much was Shaw's attention centred on his general theme that he first composed the play in the abstract, with no particular setting or character names, and then applied to Sidney Webb for a suitable war, being thereupon informed that the Serbo-Bulgarian one of 1885 was what he wanted.

Shaw was prepared to sketch in the local colour after the fact, but it was quite otherwise with the military details. These he researched elaborately and was able to quote chapter and verse when they were questioned, at the same time insisting that the play's wider subject was the collision of complex reality, 'free from creeds and systems', with conventional, romantic illusions, especially those heroic attitudes fostered by the theatre. Reality is represented by Bluntschli, the Swiss professional soldier, illusion by the Bulgarians. 'In this dramatic scheme', Shaw wrote, stressing the theatrical metaphor, 'Bulgaria may be taken as symbolic of the stalls on the first night of a play. The Bulgarians are dramatic critics; the Swiss is the realist playwright invading this realm'.[4] However Shaw's confident assertion must be taken somewhat guardedly, for *Arms and the Man* follows the pattern of *Widowers' Houses* and *Mrs Warren's Profession*: its first confrontation focuses brilliantly on a specific social issue, after which the play becomes more elusive than the forceful opening would lead one to expect.

The moment that Bluntschli, fleeing for his life, enters Raina's bedroom, the conflict between the realistic and romantic view of soldiering begins. To the fugitive's assurance that he does not mean to be killed if he can help it, the idealistic girl replies scornfully, 'Some soldiers, I know, are afraid to die'. At this point Bluntschli presents a double response, the mechanism of which is worth noticing, for it suggests how Shaw's humour projects his ideas by effecting a reversal of values. The conduct that Raina has stigmatised as exceptional cowardice Bluntschli converts to universal virtue: 'All of them, dear lady, all of them, believe me'. In performance the actress playing Raina must react with displeasure at the collapse of her values, and the well-meaning soldier offers her a supposedly consolatory explanation: 'It is our duty to live as long as we can'. But the consolation is false and the explanation a mockery, for the supposed idealistic obligation, duty, is obviously only a playful disguise for the natural desire for life. Shaw plays variations on his joke throughout the act. Thus, for example, Bluntschli's insistent classification of soldiers as old (those who carry food and who in the charge avoid trying to fight) or young (those who carry pistols and cartridges and slash with their swords) is a substitute for Raina's traditional grouping of them as brave (Bulgarians) or cowardly (Serbs): 'You must excuse me: [when Bluntschli confesses his nervousness after three days under fire] our soldiers are not like that'. Even Bluntschli's comments on Sergius' cavalry charge are a whimsical attempt to substitute his practical values for Raina's heroic, that is to say theatrical ones: 'It's no use, dear lady: I cant make you see it from the professional point of view'.

Although the first act of *Arms and the Man* focuses primarily on the military theme, there are hints of other matters, such as the good-humoured satire of Bulgarian behaviour (Raina boasts that people of high social standing in her country 'wash their hands nearly every day'), which is in fact a satire of the British idealising of a peasantry only recently liberated from Turkish domination. More significant, however, are the roles that Bluntschli and Raina play as their relationship alters during the act. They are to be happily engaged by the end of the play, but there is very little of the erotic here. Bluntschli begins as, in effect, a wise parent firmly enlightening a child who does not understand the realities of the world (in this role he fulfils a function similar to that of Sartorius and Mrs Warren). But as his fatigue grows and as Raina resolves to help him, their roles are to a considerable degree reversed. Bluntschli becomes less able to cope and more childlike: 'Forgive me: I'm too tired to think. . . . Dont scold me'. 'I forgot. It might make you cry', replies Raina, who has already been described as stooping over the disheartened Bluntschli *'almost maternally'* and who at the end of the act protects him as if he were an exhausted child who had been put to bed: 'Dont mamma: the poor darling is worn out. Let him sleep'.

With the first act concluded, Shaw, still following the pattern of *Widowers' Houses* and *Mrs Warren's Profession*, has largely presented his explicit social theme, but the personal comedy remains to be worked out. On the surface it takes the form of a traditional intrigue devoted to the unsuccessful attempt to conceal from Raina's father and her fiancé her rescue of Bluntschli. In addition it becomes an exposure of further romantic extravagances, those of the 'higher love'. Since both Raina and Sergius (modelled on Shaw's acquaintance, the writer, adventurer, and socialist member of Parliament, R. B. Cunninghame Graham) have from the first had grave doubts about the exalted attitudes they have been assuming, the task is not a very difficult one, though Shaw gets a good deal of comic mileage out of it. More to the point, however, is the relationship between Sergius and Louka. It is characterised by passion, jealousy, quarrelsomeness, and struggles for sexual power. Louka is right when she says to Sergius (who in a burst of anger has called her a 'clod of common clay'), 'whatever clay I'm made of, youre made of the same'. In contrast is the relationship between Bluntschli and Raina which, for all the genuine romantic charm that Shaw evokes as Raina finally accepts her 'chocolate cream soldier', is characterised less by erotic attraction than by a variation on the pedagogical impulse already seen in Act I. By refusing to believe in her 'noble attitude' and 'thrilling voice', Bluntschli teaches Raina not the reality of her self – she has known that all along – but the reality of proper behaviour in the world. And his reward for performing this parental function is that Raina abruptly sits beside him with '*babyish familiarity*'.

The other surrogate parent in the play, who also instructs a young woman on wordly behaviour, is Nicola, the disquietingly amenable servant who seems as content to see Louka as his customer as to have her for his wife. He and Bluntschli are linked by Bluntschli's admiration for him – 'Nicola's the ablest man Ive met in Bulgaria' – and by the fact that Shaw gives them the same joke, the conversion of a characterological insult into a commendation: told by Louka that he has the soul of a servant, Nicola replies, 'Yes: thats the secret of success in service'; told by Raina that he thinks of things that would not enter a gentleman's mind, Bluntschli answers calmly, 'Thats the Swiss national character, dear lady'. The strategy in both cases is to make a virtue of what is by the standards of the common world a defect. It is the peculiarly emotiveless quality of that virtue which leads each of them to evoke in the other characters a similar sense of astonishment: as to whether Nicola is base or heroic, as to whether Bluntschli is heroic or human: 'What a man! Is he a man?'

This curious relationship between the firmly professional soldier and the bloodlessly efficient household servant is crucial to the quality of Shaw's success in *Arms and the Man*. He is able to write its engagingly happy ending with the love match between Bluntschli and Raina because he has displaced onto Nicola the most noticeable aspects of the emotional remoteness and the asexuality that are so often disquieting elements in the Shavian hero. Compared to the ease with which Nicola gives up his sexual interest in Louka for a commercial one (his age has in any case made the relationship seem almost incestuous) the calmness with which Bluntschli hears of the death of his father (in this connection see Shaw's strangely dispassionate letter to Mrs Patrick Campbell on the cremation of his mother) can pass as little more than manly restraint.[5] By contrast with the torments and persistent disillusions of Sergius, Bluntschli's calm self-sufficiency seems altogether admirable. And finally, just as the corruption and limitations of her world led Vivie Warren to withdraw from it to a different realm, so – with everything translated to comic terms – the ignorance, the foolishness, the disturbing passions of the commonplace world of Bulgaria are left behind as Bluntschli and Raina withdraw to Switzerland, their new world of efficiency, democratic equality, and domesticity without illusions.

The stripping away of illusions from domesticity is a subject, perhaps the central subject, of one of the richest, most attractive, and most elusive of Shaw's earlier plays. *Candida* was begun in October of 1894, the time at which the initial stage direction sets it, and finished before the end of the year. When no English production appeared imminent, Shaw recommended it to Richard Mansfield, who had had some moderate success in America with *Arms and the Man*. Unfortunately, he also recommended his friend Janet Achurch for the part of Candida, and Mansfield incautiously engaged her. When she appeared in New York, he took an intense dislike to her, protesting to Shaw that he could not make love to such a Candida even if he anaesthetised himself with ether. More important was his judgement that the play would not succeed, though he professed to admire and appreciate it. 'You'll have to write a play that a *man* can play', he wrote to Shaw, 'and about a woman that heroes have fought for and a bit of ribbon that a knight tied to his lance'.[6] That an actor who had just played Bluntschli could write such quaint falderal to the author of *The Philanderer*, with its denigration of the manly man and the womanly woman, must have confirmed for Shaw the distance that still separated him from his public and his performers. In 1897 Janet Achurch took *Candida* to the English provinces and in 1900 gave a single performance in London with Granville-Barker as Marchbanks. Finally, after *Candida* had been immensely successful in Arnold Daly's New York production of 1903, it took a prominent place in Barker's Shaw repertoire at the Royal Court.

Candida's initial difficulties are, to some degree, surprising since the play not only belonged to a familiar genre but seemed, at first, not to violate that genre's conventions. On the manuscript Shaw entitled his work 'A Domestic Play in Three Acts'; specifically, *Candida* belonged to a widespread mode of domestic comedy in which the wife of a seemingly prosaic husband is tempted by a more dashing or sensitive lover but eventually finds admirable qualities in her husband that lead her to stay with him.[7] Even Ibsen had produced an example of this pattern in *The Lady from the Sea*. The Shavian variation in *Candida* was to make the source of the wife's faithfulness not her sudden discovery of a husband's strength but her long-standing recognition of his weakness. (So attractive was this view that *Candida* fathered, or rather mothered such examples of 'feminist' sentimentality as J. M. Barrie's *What Every Woman Knows* and Robert Anderson's *Tea and Sympathy*.) Fifty years after writing *Candida* Shaw himself emphasised the theme of male weakness, and suggested a different dramatic progenitor, in claiming that his play was 'a counterblast to Ibsen's *Doll's House*, showing that in the real typical doll's house it is the man who is the doll'.[8]

But Shaw had placed the emphasis elsewhere in the subtitle he gave to the published version of the play – 'A Mystery' – and in his assertion in the Preface to the *Pleasant Plays* that Candida was 'a modern pre-Raphaelite play'. Whether the term 'Mystery' refers to the secret that at the end of the play the poet has in his heart and that the husband and wife do not know, or whether, as seems more likely, it indicates the play's genre as a modern version of the medieval mystery play, evidently celebrating Candida as Madonna, the subtitle shifts the focus to include lover and wife. It is, one assumes, this element of medievalism that led Shaw to associate his play with Pre-Raphaelitism, but his comments on this matter in the Preface are far from helpful, for there he appears to be confounding the Pre-Raphaelite painters and poets with the Christian Socialist clergymen such as Morell in the play. The explanation that he seems to offer at one moment in the Preface turns out to be no explanation at all: 'To distill the quintessential drama from Pre-Raphaelitism, medieval or modern, it must be shewn at its best in conflict with the first broken, nervous, stumbling attempts to formulate its own revolt against itself as it develops into something higher'.[9] Shaw seems to suggest that Marchbanks is Morell at a more exalted stage of Pre-Raphaelite development, but Morell is not a Pre-Raphaelite, at least in any specific sense, and Marchbanks may not be either. All that they really have in common, aside from the fact that the poet and the parson both deal in words, is their mutual infatuation with Candida.

Shaw may well have been using the term *Pre-Raphaelite* here as a private code-word for what he felt to be the general religious impulse of the age, which he was formulating for himself as the doctrine of the Life Force. If so, his persistent references to Candida as the Virgin Mother suggest that he saw her as an embodiment of feminine power of vital creativity.[10] This notion is furthered by the portrait of the Virgin (Candida as presiding goddess of the household) over the mantelpiece, presented by Marchbanks because of its supposed resemblance to his beloved. Originally Shaw had specified Raphael's 'Sistine Madonna', but in the published play he substituted a detail from Titian's 'Assumption of the Virgin'. Morgan quotes a Shavian-seeming phrase from Berenson, which Shaw might well have seen, describing the Titian Madonna as 'borne up by the fullness of life within her.'[11] That the Titian is a peculiar combination of exalted power and eroticism (the centre of the picture is a great fold of drapery heavily knotted over the genital region, at once barrier and emphasis) is also appropriate to the Candida of the play, whom Beatrice Webb described as a 'sentimental prostitute' and whom Shaw himself, in a more impatient mood, called 'that very immoral female Candida'. 'She seduces Eugene', he continued, 'just exactly as far as it is worth her while to seduce him. She is a woman without "character" in the conventional sense. Without brains and strength of mind she would be a wretched slattern and voluptuary. She is straight for natural reasons, not for conventional ethical ones. Nothing can be more coldbloodedly reasonable than her farewell to Eugene'.[12] But Shaw is no clearer when baiting the 'Candidamaniacs' than when exalting his creation. Within a few sentences here Candida the 'immoral' seductress becomes an exemplar of 'natural' straightness and then one who 'coldbloodedly' disposes of an inconvenient lover. That Shaw's comments on Candida are so contradictory suggests how deeply divided his feelings were about the character he had created and the various aspects of femininity she embodied; that his comments on the play as a whole are hardly more lucid suggests that this simply-constructed domestic drama takes its readers and spectators out into deeper waters than its modest scale might lead them to expect.

One way of approaching the difficulties of *Candida* is to start with the lesser characters: Prossy, Lexy, and Burgess. Not surprisingly they perform the functions usual for such figures in the drama: they help provide information; they act as foils to the major characters; they offer comic relief. In the opening exchange between Prossy and Morell, for example, all three elements appear. The invitation to address the Hoxton Freedom Group, 'half a dozen ignorant and conceited costermongers without five shillings between them' in Prossy's dismissive words, reveals the extent of Morell's career as a public speaker for liberal causes. It also plays off Prossy's conventional disparagement of the merchants against Morell's kindly, if slightly self-conscious acceptance of their pretensions as he determines to forego a City dinner to address them. And finally Shaw offers a semi-private joke at his own expense as Morell finds to his annoyance that a likely date for the Hoxton costermongers has been pre-empted for a group less to his liking: 'Bother the Fabian Society!'

The humour is always a significant element which Shaw uses to work variations on the serious material. Thus Morell's earnest enthusiasm at the supposed conversion of Burgess to a 'moddle hemployer' collapses instantly as it becomes clear that Burgess has only changed his ways to get his 'contrax assepted'. The comic undercutting of Morell's moral certainty anticipates the psychological undercutting of his husbandly assurance with regard to

Candida. Even Burgess' mistaken assumptions – that Marchbanks has *delirium tremens* and 'must leave it off grajally' or that the members of the Morell household are mad – point whimsically to the emotional centre of the play: those accused of madness – Morell, Candida, Marchbanks, and Proserpine – are those entangled in the love relationships.

Shaw's dramatic instincts finally led him to make the lesser figures into comically fragmented or distorted echoes of the major ones. Lexy Mill, like Marchbanks, is a young man of superior status – expressed humorously on stage by a finicky accent – who thinks Candida 'extremely beautiful' and is treated by Morell in an affectionately paternal manner. Burgess is, like Morell, a father; even more to the point he is a successful man, immersed in practical affairs whose claims to dignity and power are continually undercut by the attacks of a rebellious son, even though that son-figure is an 'otherworldly' person whose views this father does not respect. In effect, the first act of *Candida* consists essentially of the same scene played twice, once comically and once seriously. The hinge upon which these episodes turn is the fact that Morell plays the son in the comic scene, the father in the serious one. Attacking one of Burgess' basic suppositions about his own character and thus removing '*the keystone of his moral arch*', Morell anticipates something of his own loss of assurance at the hands of Marchbanks. The attack on Burgess by Prossy – 'silly old fathead' – is the most notable example in the play of comic transformation. Candida's assaults must be conducted under the guise of maternal solicitude, but Proserpine's can be allowed into the open because they are funny. The two women are thus related by more than their unusual names and by more even than Prossy's desire to take Candida's place in the

Morell household. Although the vividness of Shaw's humour saves Prossy from exemplifying the kind of sentimentality the Viennese call *Hausmeisterschmerz*, she is a classic example of the younger woman, usually a maid or governess, who feels the pain of unsatisfied longing for the master of the house. The range of Shaw's empathy (or the extent of his neuroses, depending on one's point of view) allows him to deal with such deep-seated childhood fantasies in both feminine and masculine terms, even as he hides them beneath the sheltering cloak of his comedy.

Nevertheless, despite the natural impulse toward comic concealment, some of the material that is so humorously transmuted with regard to the lesser figures of the play becomes more nearly explicit in the attitudes and actions of the major ones. In recognising its nature, one recognises also the kind of ambiguous 'happiness' that Marchbanks ultimately understands he must forego. Before he comes to that understanding, however, Marchbanks – and the spectators – have a considerable distance to travel. The confident assertion of his love in the first act becomes by the end of the play a troubled negation. But the play is by no means a simple progression. Marchbanks' Act I confrontation with Morell is a curious mixture of elements, some of which anticipate later revelations, others of which are contradicted by them. The first accusation that Marchbanks directs at Morell is instructive for what is erroneous about it as much as for what is correct. Accusing Morell of exploiting Candida, Marchbanks says, 'you have selfishly and blindly sacrificed her to minister to your self-sufficiency'. Justified in recognising that Morell has thoughtlessly accepted his wife's supportive labour, Marchbanks is quite wrong in thinking that Candida has been sacrificed, much less by Morell's volition: she has been the guiding force in establishing the arrangements and has been amply repaid with household power. In general, Marchbanks tends to be shrewd about Morell (seeing the limitations in his notions of domestic happiness, recognising that his preaching does not really interest his wife) but less so in idealising Candida as 'a great soul, craving for reality, truth, freedom'.

In the next act Marchbanks learns more about Candida, as do Morell and the spectators. Under the guise of wifely solicitude she confirms to her husband Marchbanks' assertion that his preaching and speechmaking are empty verbalising and adds the accusation that they amount to little more than unconscious sexual exhibitionism stimulating to women in his audience: 'Theyre all in love with you. And you are in love with preaching because you do it so beautifully. And you think it's all enthusiam for the kingdom of Heaven on earth; and so do they. You dear silly!' The destructive sense of her words is masked by their tone of maternal affection, but even that affection seems qualified a moment later as Candida muses on whether she should give herself to Marchbanks lest he learn 'what love really is' from 'a bad woman'. Although Candida protests that she will not do so because of her love for her husband, she couples her protestation with a further denigration of his talents: 'Put your trust in my love for you, James; for if that went, I should care very little for your sermons: mere phrases that you cheat yourself and others with every day'.

From one point of view, that of the child/intruder, these scenes constitute a gratifying oedipal fantasy. The father figure is shown to be weak (in effect, he is emasculated), and the mother's sexual interest is directed towards the son. But the fantasy itself is now threatening, for incestuous fulfilment – even imaginative fulfilment – is hardly allowable. Some mode of release from its dangers must be found. Candida, not understanding the depth of

Morell's fears about Marchbanks, invites the others to share her amusement over what she takes to be his shock at her unconventionality. Shaw describes Marchbanks' reaction to Morell's distress in a striking stage direction: '*Eugene looks, and instantly presses his hand on his heart, as if some pain had shot through it*'. In the Introduction to his edition of *Candida*, Raymond S. Nelson observes that the pose is taken from *Parsifal* and suggests that it reveals Marchbanks to have, in common with Wagner's 'pure fool', a 'sensitivity to human suffering'.[13] It does so, but it also reveals a good deal more than that. Shaw does seem to have associated *Parsifal* with *Candida,* for the letter to Ellen Terry of 6 April 1896, which contains the designation of Candida as Virgin Mother, also has a reference to Parsifal as pure fool a few lines earlier. The moment alluded to in Marchbanks' pose is the climax of Parsifal's temptation in the magic garden; by empathising with the wounded father/king figure – 'Amfortas, die Wunde' – Parsifal saves himself from succumbing to the wiles of the mother/enchantress through whose enticements Amfortas has fallen to his present condition. Like Marchbanks, Parsifal must reject fleshly entanglements and depart on a pilgrimage leading ultimately to a more spiritual state. The explicitness of Shaw's stage direction suggests he was conscious of his Wagnerian allusion, but it is doubtful that he allowed himself to recognise its full resonance or that he caught in his own heroine's name the hint of Wagner's maternal temptress, Kundry.[14]

Another Wagnerian allusion appears glancingly in Act III when, left alone with Candida, Marchbanks evokes an episode in *The Twilight of the Gods* as he tells her that if he were 'a hero of old' he would have lain his 'drawn sword' between them. Though this opera was not consciously meaningful for Shaw, and the symbols operating in the dialogue at this point in the play are also traditional religious and sexual ones, the element of prohibition in a special triangular relation (also the central motif in *Tristan and Isolde*) is inescapable. Marchbanks is now allowed to address Candida by her first name and implies that each utterance of that name is 'prayer' addressed to her. When asked by Candida if he desires more than the happiness of being able to pray thus, he replies, 'No: I have come into heaven, where want is unknown'. Later, he insists to Morell in a burst of poetic enthusiasm, that Candida had offered him all he requested: 'her shawl, her wings, the wreath of stars on her head, the lilies in her hand, the crescent moon beneath her feet –'. But all of this 'Virgin Mother' imagery had reached its erotic climax a few lines earlier when Marchbanks described to Morell what had happened when he 'approached the gate of Heaven at last': 'Then she became an angel; and there was a flaming sword that turned every way, so that I couldnt go in; for I saw that that gate was really the gate of Hell'. The Biblical imagery of this passage barely masks its sexual content. Despite Marchbanks' claim that Candida refused to let him 'go in', his own revulsion from 'the gate of Hell' is the most powerful factor here.

That Marchbanks' rejection of an active sexual role precedes Candida's final revelation is significant, for it suggests that the fears and prohibitions evoked by the 'flaming sword' are the primary source of his refusal. But although the incest taboo is already firmly established before Candida's final revelations, they are a significant factor in determining his departure. Candida's claim that she has been Morell's 'mother and three sisters and wife and mother to his children all in one' is both a request that the extent of her affectionate labours be recognised and an assertion of domestic and psychic power. Earlier in the scene Marchbanks had angrily questioned Candida's statement that Morell was master in the house: 'By what right is he master?' Asked to explain, Morell had offered a reply that was, by feminist principles, impeccable: 'My dear: I don't know of any right that makes me master. I assert no such right'. Now Candida, detailing her care of him, explains: 'I make him master here, though he does not know it, and could not tell you a moment ago how it came to be so'. But Candida's explanation is in fact an insistence, under the very thinnest of disguises, that she is master. It passes on stage because of Candida's charm of utterance and Morell's immediate acceptance of her as 'the sum of all loving care', but when she asks Marchbanks if she is mother and sisters to him, he senses the danger of domination and rises *'with a fierce gesture of disgust'* exclaiming 'Out, then, into the night with me!'

It is this acceptance of exile from the world of human happiness that confirms Marchbanks' status as the stronger of the two men. Not only is he strong enough to endure the lack of what Morell must have, but he rejects it as unworthy. When Shaw later explained the final stage direction that Candida and Morell do not know *'the secret in the poet's heart'*, he identified it with Marchbanks' assertion that he no longer desires happiness (Candida had said only that he had learnt to live without it): 'life is nobler than that'. A poet, Shaw said, has no business 'with the small beer of domestic comfort and cuddling and petting at the apron-string of some dear nice woman'.[15] Shaw here equates, as trivial matters, 'domestic comfort' and domestic affection (perhaps sexuality in general), suggesting that 'cuddling and petting' involve reduction to the level of the woman's apron-string, that is to the size and condition of the child. Refusing such pleasures and limitations, the poet accepts, in effect, Carlyle's imperative: 'there is in man a Higher than Love of Happiness: he can do without Happiness, and instead thereof find Blessedness!'[16] But the state of Blessedness, as Marchbanks is to experience it, involves the rejection of the world of ordinary human concerns for the realm of 'Tristan's holy night' (as Shaw put it in the letter to Huneker already quoted from), a visionary world of supreme romantic ecstasy and death.

That the symbolic withdrawal to some such realm was a characteristic Shavian act is hardly to be doubted. It will recur again and again in Shaw's work, and indeed an anticipation of it has already appeared in Vivie Warren's absolute removal of herself from emotional and worldly entanglements. But the opposing view is also Shavian. Candida's charms, though they have darker aspects, are not the disguises of a Strindbergian monster-woman but allurements created by a playwright whose nature was deeply sensitive to them. The questions raised in the play about the efficacy of Morell's socialist activities go beyond the vanities of the individual character and touch on Shaw's ultimate doubts about the human capacity for rational political reform. But Shaw never wavered in his moral commitment to doing necessary work in the world; Morell is as much his surrogate there as Marchbanks is his vicar in a realm of more exalted aspiration. Morell had at first ridiculed Marchbanks' love because of the difference between his age and Candida's, but at the very end of the play Candida offers Marchbanks a version of the same theme, now in a dignified, lyrical vein: 'When I am thirty, she will be forty-five. When I am sixty, she will be seventy-five'. The desire to bridge the immutable gap between the limitations of reality and the dream of fulfilment remains always a central Shavian impulse.

In his 'Virgin Mother' letter to Ellen Terry (6 April 1896)

Shaw referred to the play that followed *Candida* as 'that atrocious "Man of Destiny," a mere stage brutality'; when he published it, he moderated his strictures sufficiently to subtitle it merely 'A Trifle'. Shaw's self-critical severity (which did not prevent him from trying, unsuccessfully, to have it produced at the Lyceum with Terry and Henry Irving) derived no doubt from the play's being so much a contrived intrigue over a stolen love letter, with even a hint of an illicit liaison at the end. It is certainly an example of the 'Sardoodledum' that Shaw was inveighing against (for comments on its relation to Sardou's Napoleon play, *Madame sans gêne*, see Chapter 3) but with considerable differences, one of which is an echo, surprising in view of the disparity in subject matter, of *Candida*. When the Strange Lady tells Napoleon, who is about to open a letter revealing Josephine's infidelity, that he is on the brink of losing his happiness, he is without concern: 'Happiness! Happiness is the most tedious thing in the world to me. Should I be what I am if I cared for happiness?' Shaw's Napoleon has learned Marchbanks' fearful lesson, but he has not withdrawn into 'Tristan's holy night', and though he has remained in the world like Morell, he has not been tied to a woman's apron string; he has been able to exert his will and function as a creature of power.

Napoleon is thus 'Shaw's first dramatization of heroism'.[17] The figure of the future Emperor must have had for Shaw a certain autobiographical resonance, for he is described as having known '*poverty, ill-luck, the shifts of impecunious shabby-gentility, repeated failure as a would be author* . . .'. Moreover, Shaw tells us that Napoleon is '*creative without religion, loyalty, patriotism or any of the common ideals*', which is to say that is without the mindless, mechanical versions of such ideals that Shaw had denounced in *The Quintessence of Ibsenism*. Napoleon is, however, like Shaw, an actor capable of assuming conventional attitudes. 'Self-sacrifice', he intones, 'is the foundation of all true nobility of character'. 'Ah', says the Strange Lady, deflating the pose with Shavian/feminine shrewdness, 'it is easy to see that you have never tried it, General'. During the duel of wit over the despatches, which is the real action of the play, the Lady recognises that the essence of Napoleon's character is precisely the reverse of what he claims. 'You can fight and conquer for yourself and for nobody else', she tells him. 'You are not afraid of your own destiny'. In the wider Shavian vision such proto-Nietzschean egotism must be tempered by self-control (which Shaw calls the 'supreme' vital sense in the Preface to *Back to Methuselah*) and ultimately by a higher purpose. Within the modest limits of the *Man of Destiny*, however, it is counterbalanced by the courage of the Lady, which is of 'no use' for her 'own purposes' but operates 'through the instinct to save and protect someone else'. Napoleon's whimsical meditation at the end of the play on the Englishman's power once he has got into his mind 'a burning conviction that it is his moral and religious duty to conquer those who possess the thing he wants' is at once a teasing criticism of bourgeois hypocrisy and a Shavian hint of what will eventually be possible to those in the grip of the Life Force.

Like *The Man of Destiny*, *You Never Can Tell* offers glimpses of Shavian vistas, but they are only seen in the background, behind a comic edifice that Shaw claimed in the Preface to the *Pleasant Plays* to have constructed to satisfy the demands by managers of fashionable West End theatres. When the play was withdrawn while in rehearsal at such a theatre (the Haymarket), because the actors thought they could not make an effect in it, Shaw must have been deeply disappointed, but he converted his distress into a good-humoured comic triumph a few years later when he contributed a chapter to the manager's theatrical memoirs in which he portrayed himself as having quite unnerved the company by appearing at rehearsal in a new suit.[18] Despite the misgivings of the Haymarket actors, the play stages well, but it remains a lesser work because in attempting to 'humanize' (Shaw's term in the Preface) the materials of a certain kind of farcical comedy (assignations in a private dining-room manipulated by a comic waiter) Shaw dissipated the old effects deriving from amorous intrigues and mistaken identities but did not manage to develop fully the Shavian alternatives. Thus Valentine, the 'duellist of sex', is not a dashing man about town (he is, however, like Charteris of *The Philanderer*, a compulsive flirt) but a love smitten dentist; though he sounds for a moment like an anticipation of Tanner as he speaks of 'Nature . . . suddenly lifting her great hand to take us . . . and use us, in spite of ourselves, for her own purposes, in her own way', these words turn out to be not an expression of a philosophy but merely a lover's ploy. And he is only a little more than conventionally nervous when his beloved ceases abruptly to be a caricature of the New Woman and becomes a marital bully instead.

However, the comedy of Don Juan as dentist is only one element in *You Never Can Tell*. In the central restaurant scene – presided over by the amiably soothing comic waiter – the confrontation is not between temporarily quarrelling lovers but between an implacably estranged husband and wife. When the irascible Mr Crampton, invited to lunch with the family of his dentist-tenant, turns out to be the long-lost husband and father, an element of traditional romance enters the play, but Shaw cannot treat it romantically. There can be no Shakespearean reconciliation here, for the remote, intellectual parent and the emotional, demanding one were dangerous figures for Shaw, evocative as they were of the deprivations of his own childhood. In *Major Barbara*, where these figures are far more richly transmuted, he was able to handle them successfully, but here Mrs Clandon is only a bluestocking and Crampton a bad tempered old gentleman easily manipulated by a clever girl, a figure treated more appealingly in Malone Sr of *Man and Superman*. Even the *deus ex machina* QC, brought on to round matters out, has little of Shavian substance to offer except the notion that a man may be as much entitled to a marriage settlement as a woman. Only the festive atmosphere of the final act manages to bring this last of the *Pleasant Plays* to what passes for a happy ending.

'Three Plays for Puritans'

In the Preface to the *Three Plays for Puritans* – written, of course, after the plays had been grouped together for publication – Shaw claimed that the commercial theatrical managers of his day, having determined that love was the only subject of universal appeal to their pleasure-seeking audience but having also found themselves debarred by the limits of decency from any 'realistic treatments of the incidents of sex', turned in desperation to 'the romantic play: that is, the play in which love is carefully kept off the stage, whilst it is alleged as the motive of all the actions presented to the audience'. Calling upon 'the Puritans' to rescue the theatre again 'as they rescued it before' (a very Shavian interpretation of what the closing of the theatres had accomplished), Shaw seems to be offering these three plays to be read as part of a campaign against the voluptuousness of an age that 'has crowned the idolatry of

Art with the deification of Love'. Characteristically, Shaw is at once playful and serious. It is difficult to suppose that Shaw thought 'Puritans' could rescue the turn-of-the-century theatre or even to know whom he might really have addressed by such a term – perhaps anyone who troubled to purchase a volume of his plays. But Shaw was deeply aware that the dangerous 'ideals' of popular morality were ensconced in popular culture generally and the theatre in particular ('Ten years of cheap reading have changed the English from the most stolid nation in Europe to the most theatrical and hysterical'); in subverting current theatrical conventions and attitudes he was, in fact, offering an alternative vision of life.

The particular conventions that he dealt with in *The Devil's Disciple* were those of melodrama, especially as it was performed at the Adelphi Theatre under the management of William Terriss. Although Shaw wrote the play, in the autumn of 1896, at Terriss' suggestion, the actor-manager did not react favourably when it was read to him, and any possibility that he would produce it, was foreclosed by his unexpected death. But Mansfield's production in the United States was a notable success, the royalties enabling Shaw to retire from journalism. In England the play was less appealing, perhaps because of the military circumstances, for it was a rule in melodrama that British forces were supposed invariably to be triumphant. (The conclusion of Dick's gallows speech, 'Amen, and God damn the King!' in the British Library manuscript became a more tactful, even Creative Evolutionary 'Amen! my life for the world's future!' in the published version.)[19] Shaw's crucial violation of the conventions of melodrama – his insistence that Dick sacrifices himself out of general human sympathy rather than for love of the heroine – was ingeniously subverted during the initial English production when the play ran for a few weeks in a London suburb: inspired by a critic's insistence that the hero was suppressing his passion out of a sense of honour, the actor playing Dick would, as Shaw explained in the Preface, slip behind the heroine and imprint 'a heart-broken kiss on a stray lock of her hair whilst he uttered the barren denial'.

But if Shaw altered one of the assumptions of melodrama, that the heroism of the leading figure was sexually motivated, he retained several other features of the genre intact. 'Every old patron of the Adelphi pit', he noted, 'would, were he not beglamored . . . [by Shaw's insistent self-advertisement] recognize the reading of the will, the oppressed orphan finding a protector, the arrest, the heroic sacrifice, the court martial, the reprieve at the last moment, as he recognizes beef-steak pudding on the bill of fare at his restaurant'. The first of these characteristics, the reading of the will, serves to introduce the 'Diabolonian' Richard and contrast his natural, 'vital' morality with the conventional, repressive Puritanism represented most strongly by his mother. Although some of the first audiences seem to have been troubled by Richard's supposed wickedness, it is difficult to believe that anyone who could recognise the good heart beneath the scapegrace exterior of Charles Surface in *The School for Scandal* would be deceived by Dick Dudgeon. (The tradition of the bandit hero whose finer sensibility has made him a social exile is most notably exemplified in Schiller's *Die Raüber*,[20] parodied in Gilbert's *The Pirates of Penzance*, and again treated playfully by Shaw in *Man and Superman*.)

What makes the first act memorable, however, is not the putative iniquity of Richard or the pathos of Essie or the comic hypocrisy of the family but the portrait of the love-denying cruelty of Mrs Dudgeon, her hatred of her son and consequent rejection by him. Although a touch of sympathy for her is produced by the knowledge that she had been bullied by the local clergyman into a loveless marriage (Ibsen's Mrs Alving, who is clearly evoked here, must have been a particularly meaningful figure for the son of Lucinda Carr Shaw, who had made so grave a mistake in her marriage to a secret drinker), Mrs Dudgeon remains a classic portrait of the Wicked Witch, the Bad Mother (the Jungian term need not be resisted here). Despite Mrs Dudgeon's rejecting nature, the action of this scene is, from one point of view at least, a fantasy of love, a kind by now familiar enough but hardly one Shaw could have recognised in 1896. A father, unmourned, though he had been kindly and protective, is certified as dead, and his son takes his place as head of the household and possessor of the mother's property.

The tendency of this oedipal material is frustrated, as it must be, by Mrs Dudgeon's nature. When, however, the fantasy is repeated in Act II, the character of the mother figure is quite different, and a new mode of frustration must be found. Richard now enters not into a 'house of children's tears' where only the devil's servant is kind to an orphan but into a benign household where the mother figure has become young and beautiful. That the paternal head of this household is a vigorous, successful clergyman deeply involved in the social concerns of his community suggests at once that Shaw is, to some degree, reworking the materials of *Candida*. And indeed the essential action that the child/intruder performs remains the same although certain circumstances of the establishment are altered. In effect the mother figure's relationships are reversed: she is now dependent on a strong, competent father figure, and it is she who is emotionally aroused when the youthful intruder appears and demonstrates his superior qualities. But these disguising factors do not conceal such similarities as, for example, the taunting of the clergyman: 'You want to preach to me. Excuse me: I prefer a walk in the rain'. There is the initial attraction of the intruder to familial acceptance and domestic happiness. Richard must, according to Shaw's stage direction '*hide a convulsive swelling of his throat*' as soon as Anderson treats him kindly. Shortly after he meditates on the attractions of the Anderson household:

> I can see the beauty and peace of this home: I think I have never been more at rest in my life than at this moment; and yet I know quite well I could never live here. It's not in my nature, I suppose, to be domesticated. But it's very beautiful: it's almost holy.

There is even a momentary reminiscence of Marchbanks' identification with Parsifal. When Judith bursts into tears, Richard feels an impulse of intense empathy, '*putting his hand to his breast as if to a wound*'.

But Richard is most like Marchbanks in his ultimate self-defining act. Although his choice is at the end of the play foiled by the conventions of melodrama, he elects to go out into something very like 'Tristan's holy night'. Putting aside the dangerous lures of domesticity as unsuited to him, Richard chooses the more exalted attractions of sainthood. 'I am as steadfast in my religion', Richard says speaking of himself and Anderson, 'as he is in his'. The nature of this religion, however, is never really defined. Clearly it is not the religion of romantic love: though Richard is prepared to perform the action of Dickens' Sidney Carton, he is not prepared to accept Judith in the role of Lucy Manette and is 'revolted' when all she can make of his explanation is the fact that he does not love her. But the explanation of why he offers his life for Anderson's is elusive: 'I have been brought up standing by the law of my own nature; and I may not go against it, gallows or no gallows'.

Towards the end of the play Anderson offers what seems to be a comment on Richard's statement as he explains to Burgoyne how he has come to appear before him as commander of the colonial militia:

> Sir! it is in the hour of trial that a man finds his true profession. This foolish young man [*placing his hand on Richard's shoulder*] boasted himself the Devil's Disciple; but when the hour of trial came to him, he found that it was his destiny to suffer and be faithful to the death. I thought myself a decent minister of the gospel of peace; but when the hour of trial came to me, I found that it was my destiny to be a man of action, and that my place was amid the thunder of the captains and the shouting.

Anderson, however, is only affirming what has been apparent from the first: that the energetic, successful parson was a man at ease with practical affairs and that Richard was a man of high sensibilities who lived apart from such concerns. (The notion that Richard is to succeed Anderson as the town clergyman is hardly to be taken seriously, but it is a playful way of confirming Richard's 'saintly' vocation.) The reader or spectator recognises, as he does at the end of *Candida*, that contradictory Shavian necessities are being dealt with through different characters. The requirement that one earn one's salvation by performing the necessary work of the world, perhaps even creating the next generation by labouring as husband and father, is met by Morell and Anderson, while a more esoteric need – to retreat from the world's tangle of social, familial, and erotic demands – is met by those who, like Marchbanks and Richard, owe their allegiance to a more exalted ideal: a mission as artist-philosopher or exemplar of a higher morality.

A figure who answers both these demands appears in the last act of *The Devil's Disciple*, though Shaw seems to have been of two minds about Burgoyne. In his 'Notes to *The Devil's Disciple*' Shaw speaks admiringly of Burgoyne's 'fastidious delicacy of sentiment, his fine spirit and humanity' and calls him a 'critical genius'; but in a letter to Ellen Terry he says, 'Burgoyne is a gentleman; and that is the whole meaning of that part of the play', going on to explain that Richard must be 'superior to gentility – that is, to the whole ideal of modern society'.[21] Burgoyne is not insensitive to Judith's hysterical outburst, 'Is it nothing to you what wicked thing you do if only you do it like a gentleman?', and certainly he has a critical view of military inefficiency from the laxity in London that leads to the defeat of his army to its incompetent marksmanship that forces him to deny Richard a firing squad in favour of being hanged 'in a perfectly workmanlike and agreeable way'. It is not only his competence but the humane, self-critical irony, which converts a necessary brutality into something 'workmanlike and agreeable', that sets Burgoyne apart from the rigid, commonplace Swindon. Recognising their affinity, Burgoyne and Richard play ironically with their circumstances: the General courteously asking Richard if twelve o'clock will suit him as a time to be hanged, Richard assuring Burgoyne, 'I shall be at your disposal then, General'. In the figure of Burgoyne, who combines some of Richard's emotional distance from the ordinary world with Anderson's competence in dealing with it, Shaw bridges the gap between them and takes a step towards the central achievement of his next play, the dramatisation of what he will later call the Superman, what at this point he calls the hero.

Written in 1898 with Johnston Forbes-Robertson in mind ('the classic actor of our day' as Shaw called him), *Caesar and Cleopatra* was conceived as a grand-scale nineteenth-century stage spectacle, though Shaw dispensed with the usual underlying Scribean intrigue, making his play 'A History' or 'chronicle' (Shaw's terms), a series of scenes presenting Caesar in various circumstances. In fact, Shaw was annoyed with Max Reinhardt, the great director of spectacles who staged the first professional production (Berlin, 1906), for using the comparatively farcical Act III while cutting the first scene of Act IV (necessary for preparing the more serious scene to come); Shaw himself omitted Act III from Forbes-Robertson's production in New York later in 1906 and in London the following year.[22] Not only did Shaw dispense with the intrigue plot, but he put aside stage heroics, 'the old demand for the incredible . . . which was supplied by bombast, inflation, and the piling of crimes on catastrophes and factitious raptures on artificial agonies' and presented instead a figure who was 'heroic in the true human fashion'.[23]

But Shaw's Caesar is more than a kindly, humorous, efficient person who speaks colloquial English most of the time, instead of theatrical rant. In the work of the German historian Theodor Mommsen, who considered Caesar a social reformer and the 'sole creative genius produced by Rome', Shaw found a counterbalance to the Shakespearean view of the great conqueror as a vain tyrant.[24] Ignoring the Caesar whose debaucheries made Suetonius describe him as 'every woman's husband and every man's wife', Shaw created a hero who 'is above fear, sickliness of conscience, malice, and the makeshifts and moral crutches of law and order which accompany them'. Although Shaw is here describing the youthful hero of Wagner's *Ring* in the 'Siegfried as Protestant' section of *The Perfect Wagnerite* (also written in 1898), he could as well be delineating the moral independence of Caesar who, Shaw says in his Notes to the play, is sufficiently original that 'in order to produce an impression of complete disinterestedness and magnanimity, he has only to act with entire selfishness'. He is thus, Shaw says, '*naturally* great'. 'Having virtue, he has no need of goodness', that is, of the prescriptions of conventional morality. Like Wagner's hero, Caesar is a higher order of man, establishing, as Shaw said about Siegfried, 'the unfettered action of Humanity doing exactly what it likes, and producing order instead of confusion thereby because it likes to do what is necessary for the good of the race'.

The Caesar whom we meet in the play does indeed have the transcendental virtue of a higher order of man, but instead of the naiveté and energy of Siegfried, he has a consciousness of age and alienation. This is the first note sounded in the play as Caesar, in his soliloquy before the Sphinx, likens himself to the great statue as an exile in the mortal world: 'I have found flocks and pastures, men and cities, but no other Caesar, no air native to me, no man kindred to me'. Although the play itself is full of humour and even farce, as Caesar leaves Alexandria at its end, one is conscious that he is returning not only to Rome but to 'the lost region' of which he spoke to the Sphinx, that is to his death. The faithful Rufio warns his master that in Rome 'there are too many daggers', while Caesar describes himself as 'ripe for the knife'. Although Dick Dudgeon is released from the death he elected by the conventions of melodrama, Caesar cannot be freed from the inexorable claims of history. The Shavian hero/saint is always to some degree an alien in the human realm and is rarely distressed at leaving it.

Before Caesar departs, however, he has certain things to accomplish. It is clear from the Prologue by the god Ra, added in 1912, that in Shaw's mind Caesar and Pompey were emblematic figures: Pompey, representative of a regressive social order (the old Rome had grown great 'through robbery of the poor') that had become morally antiquated ('he talked of law and duty'), Caesar of a new progressive Rome smiled upon by the gods ('the way of the gods is the way of life'). But Shaw did not, in fact, bring any sense of historical movement into the play itself. When the murder of Pompey is referred to, it becomes simply an occasion for demonstrating Caesar's moral sensibility, his superiority to mere vengeance: 'Am I Julius Caesar, or am I a wolf, that you fling me the grey head of the old soldier, the laurelled conqueror, the mighty Roman, treacherously struck down by this callous ruffian, and then claim my gratitude for it!' Rebuked for his past brutalities, Caesar now rejects the 'duty of statesmanship' that had led him to commit them and, rising above anger, offers Pompey's slayer a place in his service. Ultimately Caesar's achievements in the play lie in just such confrontations as this for they allow him to perform the real dramatic mission Shaw has assigned him: to demonstrate the qualities of grace, dispassionate intelligence, and moral eminence that mankind must develop and that are notably lacking in the human creatures – some weak, some vicious, some even endearing – who surround him.

Brittanus, for example, is an appealing conceit: a nineteenth-century, middle-class Englishman incongruously present in pre-Christian Alexandria as the slave-secretary of Caesar, with whose values his own are always in feeble contrast. Sometimes the contrast is playful as when he implores Caesar, about to leap into the harbour, not to appear in the fashionable part of Alexandria till he has changed his clothes; sometimes it is more significant, as when he tries to convince Caesar that it is a point of honour to pursue those who have plotted against him, only to be told, 'I do not make human sacrifices to my honour, as your Druids do'. Another figure who identifies himself even more ostentatiously as a visitor from the nineteenth century is Apollodorus, the patrician carpet vendor, who explains his occupation to a doubting Roman sentry: 'I do not keep a shop. Mine is a temple of the arts. I am a worshipper of beauty. . . . My motto is Art for Art's sake'. Apollodorus is not only a *fin de siècle* aesthete, but a romantic lover, an idealiser of woman's beauty, Cleopatra's 'perfect knight', who assures her, in appropriately high-flown language, that should they have to face death 'she shall not want the devotion of a man's heart and the strength of a man's arm'. Significantly, Cleopatra can only sob, 'But I don't want to die' and Caesar mourn sadly, 'Oh, ignoble, ignoble!' For Cleopatra, the most important of the portraits in the gallery through which Caesar moves, is in all essentials his opposite. Childish, wilful, sensual, even savage, she embodies the human characteristics Caesar has overcome. Inevitably, the child-parent relationship that she enters into with Caesar is a complex one. Any erotic quality in it is deeply submerged, though Caesar, who confesses that he is (like his creator) attracted to women and given to idealising them, is disturbed when Cleopatra, after indulging in a fantasy of whipping her 'young kings' to death when she is tired of them, tells him he will always be her 'good old king'. 'Oh, my wrinkles, my wrinkles!' he exclaims, 'And my child's heart! You will be the most dangerous of all Caesar's conquests'. Cleopatra too is disturbed by Caesar, flying into a jealous rage when he is kind to her sibling. (When Shaw turns again to the teacher/father, student/daughter relationship in *Pygmalion*, the erotic element is nearer the surface, and he has much more difficulty in disposing of it.) Though Shaw is at pains to deny his audience what his title seems to promise, 'a story of an unchaste woman' as Ra calls it in the Prologue, he does offer a conflict full of emotion. It is a development of the material Shaw had begun to work with in *You Never Can Tell*: the rivalry between two kinds of parents in the raising of a child. With the greatest economy, the play sketches in Ftatateeta's maternal devotion to her 'nursling', so passionate that she gladly becomes Cleopatra's instrument of murder. Though their relationship is founded on love, it results in authoritarian bullying (on both sides) and a continuing power struggle as to who is 'mistress of the Queen's household'. In Act I Caesar explicitly undertakes Ftatateeta's task, claiming he is perhaps 'a sorcerer' and can 'make a woman' of Cleopatra. He so far succeeds that in her Act IV confrontation with Pothinus, she is allowed a momentary echo of Eugene Marchbanks. Now that Caesar has made her wise, she says, 'I do what must be done, and have no time to attend to myself. That is not happiness; but it is greatness'. Whatever Caesar has, in fact, achieved with Cleopatra, it was not done through love, as Cleopatra explains when Pothinus asks if Caesar does not love her:

Love me! Pothinus: Caesar loves no one. Who are those we love. Only those whom we do not hate: all people are strangers and enemies to us except those we love. But it is not so with Caesar. He has no hatred in him: he makes friends with everyone as he does with dogs and children. His kindness to me is a wonder: neither mother, father, nor nurse have ever taken so much care for me, or thrown open their thoughts to me so freely.

When Pothinus suggests that this is love, Cleopatra points out that Caesar will do as much for anyone. 'His kindness is not for anything in me:' she explains, 'it is in his own nature'. (Caesar's moral superiority is, as the last phrase suggests, akin to Dick Dudgeon's.)

To Cleopatra human relations, dominated by alienation and hatred, are relieved only by impulses of sexuality. Caesar is prone to none of these feelings, but he does not distinguish between particular adults and children and dogs. This 'heroic' benevolence is profoundly attractive in its universality and almost equally disquieting in its remoteness from the individual qualities of the human creatures it so lightly touches. Even in Caesar, whose gentle humour is so ingratiating, there is a hint of the impersonality and condescension that make the Ancients of *Back to Methuselah* such forbidding figures. But whereas mankind must accept the tutelage of the Ancients, Cleopatra learns relatively little from Caesar. (Remediation is always pedagogically uncertain.) The limits of her acquirements are demonstrated in the two symetrically placed killings that are the final significant actions of the play. The murder of Pothinus, instigated by Cleopatra for vengeance, is greeted by Caesar with repulsion and a longing that the gods (anticipating the work of the Life Force) may 'create a race that can understand'. But the killing of Ftatateeta by Rufio, as a precaution and without anger or moral judgement, receives Caesar's approval. Although Cleopatra is easily appeased by Caesar's promise to send her Mark Antony, she remains Ftatateeta's violent, passionate nursling, and since she has 'taken the powers of life and death', that is Caesar's powers, upon herself, Caesar has no place in the human world of Egypt and must return to Rome and his death.

When Shaw set out, in May of 1899, to write a play for Ellen Terry, he turned again to much of the material he had worked with in *Caesar*: a conqueror travelling to Africa, who triumphs by the strength of moral superiority and shows the other characters how to rise above vengeance. But whereas Caesar leads an army, Lady Cicely Waynflete conquers exclusively through shrewdness, strength of will, and manipulative maternal charm. In one of the letters (8 August 1899) in which he attempted, vainly at that time, to persuade Ellen Terry to undertake the role, he claimed it was 'a part which dominates a play because the character it represents dominates the world' (at the point where the false ideals of Imperialism meet 'the fanatical African') and that *Captain Brassbound's Conversion* was the first play in which he had not 'prostituted the actress more or less by making the interest in her partly a sexual interest'. The very extravagance of the first claim suggests one of the central weaknesses in the play: for a work by Shaw it is thin in intellectual substance, the family revenge motif involving little more than a misunderstanding and the adventure-melodrama remaining obstinately stagey and devoid of any conflict of values. The second claim is also dubious, for Lady Cicely trades a great deal on her femininity in managing the men, all more or less bumbling, about her. Although she does avoid being merely an upper-class bully (she comes dangerously close, and only an actress of notable personal grace can carry off the role), she lacks Caesar's ease and assurance as a representative of the higher morality. Part of the problem is that in her social position she must substitute womanly manipulativeness for the power on which Caesar can ultimately rely, and part is that she is pulled too strongly by the emotional currents of the play for her dispassionate superiority to remain finally convincing. When Lady Cicely converts Brassbound from his commitment to avenge his mother, she inevitably becomes a substitute for the passionate, violent, drunken creature who had been an object of both devotion and repulsion for her son. When Lady Cicely rescues him from the court martial, she becomes available not only as an alternative to the emotionally demanding parent (we return to the theme of *You Never Can Tell* and *Caesar*) but as a possible mistress or wife. Pressed by Brassbound to marry him, Lady Cicely confesses that her power lies in the emotional distance from those around her: 'I have never been in love with any real person: and I never shall. How could I manage people if I had that mad little bit of self left in me? Thats my secret'. Lady Cicely does not say whether or not she has been in love with fantasy figures, as her creator preferred to be or had to be (beginning with his mother and continuing through Ellen Terry and beyond). Brassbound's assertion that in revealing herself Lady Cicely has restored his sense of purpose in life will not bear much consideration, though it passes muster on stage as the play swirls to Lady Cicely's serio-comic line: 'How glorious! And what an escape!' Lady Cicely's revelation may not be, as Brassbound claims it is, the 'secret of command', but it is one of the secrets of Shaw's art, which has from the first dealt not only with the comedy of social and intellectual conflicts but in richly symbolic ways with many of the intractable demands of familial relationships.

5
Plays of Maturity

The Initial Group

The plays of Shaw's first period are, inevitably, of variable quality – it would be a daring critic indeed who could argue that *The Philanderer* was of equal significance with *Candida* or *Caesar and Cleopatra* – but none of them can be ignored by anyone who wants to understand Shaw fully. Each is a major effort, and whatever its degree of artistic success, each reveals some fresh aspect of the evolving Shavian *Weltanschauung*. But in the great second period of Shaw's productivity, from 1901 to 1923, he wrote some plays over which we need not linger. There are minor sketches, occasional pieces, lesser efforts that in a book of reasonable proportions may be ignored or mentioned briefly. The first play Shaw wrote after *Captain Brassbound's Conversion*, for example, is *The Admirable Bashville*, dashed off in January of 1901 to protect his copyright in his novel *Cashel Byron's Profession*. A blank verse rendering of the book, it touches on the Shavian

134

theme of eugenics in the union of a highbrow lady and a prize-fighter, but all of its fun – and in the theatre there is a fair amount for an indulgent audience – lies in the comic incongruity between the modern (1882) setting and the pseudo-Elizabethan English (spiced with a few lines lifted from Shakespeare and Marlowe). One of the remarkable things about Shaw's output, however, is that in the surge of Shavian fecundity there are relatively few trivialities of this sort. In his period of maturity, plays such as *Major Barbara, Pygmalion, Heartbreak House,* and *Saint Joan* are only the higher peaks of a mountain range that has many notable elevations. The best view of the whole is from one of the highest of these: the play in which Shaw made publicly explicit the system of thought that had come to underlie his work and thus presented himself as a philosopher–artist.

Man and Superman

Although *Man and Superman* offers the spectator or reader manifold delights, for Shaw's invention is here at its highest, it also poses notable problems not only in terms of its intellectual and emotional substance but also with regard to its form. When Shaw published the play in 1903, it was a substantial book, including as it did the lengthy 'Epistle Dedicatory' to A. B. Walkley, Act III with the *Don Juan in Hell* section, and the appended *Revolutionist's Handbook.* But the performing version used by Granville-Barker at the Royal Court in 1905 and sanctioned by Shaw consisted only of Acts I, II, and IV, seeming to leave the play 'a trumpery story of modern London Life' (as Shaw called it in the 'Epistle') in which a clever girl pursues and catches the eligible bachelor of her choice, rather than the extraordinary drama-discourse that in its complete form it assuredly is. The discrepancy here raises a number of questions. Is the courtship comedy of Acts I, II, and IV a notable play in itself? Is it, on the other hand, a modestly attractive comedy of manners loosely attached to 'Shavio-Socratic' dialogue of essentially abstract, intellectual interest? Since the courtship comedy and the *Don Juan in Hell* scene are theatrically viable apart from each other, what, if anything, is gained as a result of the heroic efforts required to perform them together?[1] These questions may perhaps be rephrased more simply as, 'What is the relationship between the two parts of the play?'

To find an answer, it will be helpful to glance back for a moment at some of the earlier plays, for though Shaw was now writing on a grander scale and making his religious and philosophic ideas explicit as part of the substance of his work, his vision as an artist (of which his efforts as a thinker are, for our purposes, a part) has remained consistent throughout. Although the plays of the first period offer only hints of the broader ideas Shaw was generating (as in the dramatisation of Caesar as Superman), they constitute a rich dramatic anticipation of the underlying pattern of *Man and Superman*. Consider, for example, the differing fates allocated to the heroes of Shaw's previous comedies of courtship. Charteris, the talkative philanderer, though he is pursued by a forceful woman, finds that like Don Juan he is to be something other than a husband and father (these roles being assigned to a surrogate). By contrast, in *You Never Can Tell*, Valentine, who boasts himself a 'duellist of sex' is nevertheless like Tanner swept up by the power of the Life Force, as Shaw was soon to call it, and despite his feeble thrashings about at the end of the play, is seized upon by the woman whose sexual potency he has awakened. Even more striking are the cases of Harry Trench in *Widowers'*

Houses and Vivie Warren. Roused by the double lures of money and a passionate woman, Trench allows himself to be captured by the world (though it is not entirely the world of sexual creativity that captures Tanner). But when similar lures, of wealth and love, are placed before Vivie, she responds as Don Juan himself might, withdrawing to her higher world of numerical calculations.

These persistent Shavian alternatives – commitment to the demands of human existence or withdrawal from them – appear also in more complex works where the claims of both are expressed within a single play. Morell's remaining in Candida's world as husband, father, and worker for socialist causes is an action less exalted but not less significant than Marchbanks' removal of himself to the other realm of 'Tristan's holy night'. Dick Dudgeon is preserved from entering this deathly realm in *The Devil's Disciple* by the exigencies of melodramatic plot; but though Dick is immune to worldly, as well as womanly appeals and quite prepared to sacrifice his life in response to a higher call, Anthony Anderson finds that it is the claims of this world rather than those of a greater one that he is fitted to answer. In all of these cases it is clear that, although Shaw's ultimate sympathies lie with the character who makes the more exalted, 'other-worldly' choice of withdrawal, there is a counterbalancing impulse to confirm a commitment to the work of the world as well. Even *Widowers' Houses* comes to a conventional 'happy' ending in which the hero achieves love and money; that both of them are tainted is almost beside the point, for in the darker Shavian vision no other kinds are to be had. The fear that socialist preaching such as Morell's or Tanner's may amount to no more than futile exhibitionism does not diminish the Shavian sense that it is in some way still essential work of the Life Force.

When Shaw came to conceive of *Man and Superman* as a 'worldly' comedy combined with an other-worldly philosophic discourse, it was natural, almost inevitable that he should dramatise in the comedy essentially the demands of an active commitment to human affairs and that in the discourse, the vast operatic quartet/moral debate that is the *Don Juan in Hell* scene, he should realise an alternative vision in which his hero rejects such claims in favour of a destiny at once exalted and disquieting.[2] Theoretically these alternatives are not so much opposites as differing aspects of the Life Force or short and long-term strategies for aiding it in its work. If Don Juan is an idealisation of 'the great man who incarnates the philosophic consciousness of life' and Ann is 'the woman who incarnates its fecundity', as Shaw put it in the Epistle, then each part of the play illustrates one of the modes through which the Life Force operates. But this scheme, which seems to suggest what Shaw consciously had in mind, does not, in fact, reflect the play that he actually wrote.

After all, the central figure of the courtship comedy is not Ann but Tanner, and the action of the play focuses not on her fecundity (hardly a viable dramatic subject in any case) but on Tanner's efforts, at once comic and desperate, to escape her power. The comedy section of *Man and Superman* is, from one point of view, a kind of sadly humorous version of *Candida* in which Tanner, endeavouring to play the role of Marchbanks, proudly announces that he has 'higher business' on hand than mere domesticity and strides out into the night, only to have Candida rush out after him and, despite his protests, drag him back into the parsonage to assume Morell's roles of husband, father, and civic 'windbag'. The central action of the comedy is thus Tanner's discovery of Ann's designs and his energetic but futile efforts to remove himself from her power as ruler of the practical world of domestic and social obligations. Similarly, the 'action' of the *Don Juan in Hell* discourse consists of Don Juan's determination – a successful one – to remove himself from the power of the Devil's world of romantic love and beauty. Listening to the 'Shavio-socratic' dialogue, we hear a familiar theme, but one played in a different key.

Man and Superman's pivotal conceit, that Tanner is a descendant of Don Juan, is validated by their family resemblance. Confronted by the demand that they accommodate themselves to the values of the world about them, both announce their allegiance to higher values and determine to withdraw themselves from the claims made upon them. That the audience rejoices in both Tanner's failure and Don Juan's success suggests how finely Shaw has balanced the differing reactions to these claims. In Tanner's defeat there is an admixture of triumph not only for Ann's vitality but for the sense of balance that overcomes the comic excesses of Tanner's own nature. In Don Juan's success there is a certain element of loss: the Devil's most severe criticism of Don Juan's departure, that 'the pursuit of the Superhuman . . . leads to an indiscriminate contempt for the human', delivered after Juan has gone, remains unanswered. Or rather, it would remain so were it not followed by Act IV with Tanner's capitulation to what may be the demands of the Life Force or more simply the lures of a charming woman. Each part of *Man and Superman* is thus a self-sustaining entity, each being in fact a version of the other in a different mode; for both dramatise the same Shavian myth, that of withdrawal from the demands of the world. The play is at its richest when both parts are taken together because one then sees most clearly the imaginative fulfilment of the impulse to transcend the world and the contradictory acceptance of the ultimate necessity to live within it. Each part, however, is sufficiently complex at least to adumbrate the dominant impulse of the other.

Thus it is absolutely essential to Shaw's overall scheme that Tanner be less than Don Juan, though he must be considerably more than the other characters in the comedy. Tanner's superiority does not lie only, or even primarily in his being a mouthpiece for Shavian doctrine. For one thing some of what he says is little more than the traditional counsel of one bachelor to another: 'It is a woman's business to get married as soon as possible, and a man's to keep unmarried as long as he can'. And the notion that young women, along with their mothers, were energetic in pursuit of that business could hardly have astonished anyone who had attended a performance of *Lady Windermere's Fan* and noted the fun Wilde had with the manoeuvres of the Duchess of Berwick and Lady Agatha. Even when Tanner does speak of woman's role as an instrument of creativity, the climactic emphasis is always on the danger to men: 'She sacrifices herself to it [her maternal vitality]: do you think she will hesitate to sacrifice you? . . . Because they have a purpose which is not their own purpose, but that of the whole universe, a man is nothing to them but an instrument of that purpose. . . . They accuse us of treating them as a mere means to our pleasure; but how can so feeble and transient a folly as a man's selfish pleasure enslave a woman as the whole purpose of Nature embodied in a woman can enslave a man?' (One can only speculate on whether Shaw's childhood experience with a mother who had a 'higher' purpose than personal love of her children finds a curious reflection here. The 'artist man' mentioned briefly by Tanner, who is free of the 'tyranny of sex' as Shaw oddly says in the Epistle, is thus imitating as well as retaliating in kind with his own creativity.)

These darker hints, however, do not really determine the tone of the comedy scenes. We admire Tanner not only because he warns us of the dangers in male–female relationships but because of the liveliness of his humorous perceptions and the superiority of his sensibility. The latter appears particularly in his relations with women, for he is as much attracted to them as he is afraid of them. When Violet is supposed to have become pregnant out of wedlock and everyone else is decorously crushed, it is Tanner who not only spouts evolutionary rhetoric about 'the completed womanhood' but has the genuinely kindly impulse to offer Violet help, money, and respect as well as to jolt Ramsden out of his tendency 'to act up to his principles' of respectability. That Tanner is made a fool of in the splendid comic reversal at the end of Act I is as much due to Violet's pettiness as to the extravagance of his enthusiasm for 'instinct' and 'motherhood'. As the revolutionary rug is pulled out from under Tanner and he collapses '*in ruins*', as Shaw's stage direction has it, the effect is not to undermine our liking for him but to strike a comic balance between his theoretical excesses on the one hand and the complacencies of the bourgeois world on the other.

Nor is Tanner any less likable in his relations with men. When Octavius protests to Ramsden that Tanner would never take advantage of his position as Ann's guardian because he 'is a man of honor, and incapable of abusing –' Tanner interrupts with self-deprecating desperation: 'Dont, Tavy: youll make me ill. I am not a man of honor: I am a man struck down by a dead hand'. (Shaw seizes the occasion to slip into the text a faint allusion to the original figure of Don Juan clutched by the icy hand of the stone guest, but the philosophic libertine is condemned not to hell for his sexual license but to marriage for his intellectual presumption.) Similarly, when confronted by Mendoza's haughty assertion that he is a brigand who lives by robbing the rich, Tanner undercuts both his captor's romantic attitudinising and his own doubtful status as a wealthy revolutionary by responding, 'I am a gentleman: I live by robbing the poor. Shake hands'. But whereas Tanner's mordant self-awareness gives him some minimal control of his own dubious status, the other men in the play blunder on in amiable ignorance, their pretentions to dignity regularly betrayed by their relations with women. Ramsden, supposedly a liberal public man but actually the guardian of traditional familial and societal values is swiftly diminished to 'Annie's Granny' as his ward exerts her charm upon him. Octavius wishes to be a poet (though he is a mere aesthete – Tanner is the philosopher-artist of the play) but succeeds only in languishing permanently as a lovelorn suitor – the same role played by the socialist brigand Mendoza, his surrogate in Act III. Hector Malone, the romantic American moralist, is under the control of his determined wife, and even Malone Sr, the capitalist entrepreneur, finds himself slipping rapidly into Violet's orbit. The lesson of the play, from one point of view at least, would seem to be that Man must become Superman to escape the dominance of women.

In this lurid Strindbergian light, however, one does not see the play with full clarity. The women here are by no means a monolithic group. Mrs Whitefield is more than willing to grant Tanner's assertion that Ann is a liar, coquette, and bully, and that, in unscrupulously using her charm on men, she is, as he puts it, 'almost something for which I know no polite name'. Yet Shaw has her do her feeble best as a matchmaker by assuring Tanner with comic earnestness that he 'cant expect perfection'. Moreover, she is touchingly affectionate with regard to Tavy (though hardly conventionally maternal with regard to Ann) in wanting to protect him from being 'trampled on and made wretched', that is married to Ann, whom she would be pleased to see Tanner's wife because 'it would serve her right'. This whimsical defusing of generational hostility is quite a different matter from Shaw's swift delineation of Violet's revenge on Ramsden's unmarried sister, for whose disapproval, she says, 'allowances' can be made whereas 'better taste' was to be expected 'from people of greater experience'.

This petty sexual triumph over a maiden lady would be quite foreign to Ann, who is manipulative but not cruel. Shaw is careful to establish the contrast between the two girls, each of whom has a secret aim: Violet's is to get money, Ann's to get love. Although Shaw might argue that the first was the more important commodity, his play is enough of a traditional romantic comedy for our sympathies to be all with Ann. We care for her not because she is '*one of the vital geniuses*', as Shaw, most dubiously, describes her in an introductory stage direction (like all such directions to be considered carefully but not accepted casually) but because she is charmingly flirtatious, clever in her own area of expertise (telling Tanner, 'you seem to understand all the things I dont understand; but you are a perfect baby in the things I do understand'), and quite touchingly vulnerable in her manipulations. After all, just as Tanner is always being collapsed '*like a pricked bladder*' at the end of his grand orations, so is Ann always being found out in her schemes ('Abyss beneath abyss of perfidy!' shrieks Tanner in frustration). They are meant for each other because they are both fallible, though they are the best elements in the 'human' comedy.

143

In the world of the damned, things are different and yet much the same. Tanner with his bumptious enthusiasm is now replaced by Don Juan with his philosophic dignity, but they share at least one trait, their loquacity. 'Never you mind him, Mr Robinson', Straker says indulgently of his employer, 'He likes to talk. We know him, don't we?' A similar kindly contempt seems to lie behind the '*universal laughter*' of the final stage direction following Ann's assurance to Tanner that he can 'go on talking'. Although no one quite laughs at Don Juan, the Devil complains of his speeches' 'intolerable length', and the Statue, bemused by Juan's 'amazing' 'flow of words', heaves a sigh of relief at his departure: 'Whew! How he does talk! Theyll never stand it in heaven'. This coincidence in the endings of Acts III and IV is not merely fortuitous (nor does it simply reflect Shaw's persistent fear that he would 'go on talking' without being listened to). What Don Juan has been affirming by withdrawing from Hell with its 'tedious, vulgar pursuit of happiness' and what Tanner has just been saying are significant echoes of other Shavian moments. Responding to the congratulations at his engagement, Tanner announces that he is 'not a happy man'. 'Ann looks happy;' he continues, 'but she is only triumphant, successful, victorious. That is not happiness, but the price for which the strong sell their happiness. What we have both done this afternoon is renounce happiness, renounce freedom, renounce tranquillity, above all, renounce the romantic possibilities of an unknown future, for the cares of a household and a family'. Although Tanner quickly veers off into a comic denunciation of conventional wedding festivities, he has just rephrased Candida's assertion, at the end of her play, that Marchbanks had 'learnt to live without happiness', a statement that in its various reworkings always suggests for Shaw a recognition of the limitations of human life.

But now domesticity, which in *Candida* had constituted a kind of ambiguous 'happiness', becomes the occasion for a renunciation of a mere romantic fulfilment of the self. Just as Marchbanks had gone out into the night to find a higher fulfilment, so Don Juan ascends to heaven to achieve a similar purpose. Abjuring 'such romantic mirages as beauty and pleasure', Don Juan resolves to leave hell, 'the home of the unreal and of the seekers for happiness' for what the Devil aptly calls 'the alternative establishment'. There, as Juan explains to Ana, 'you live and work instead of playing and pretending. You face things as they are; you escape nothing but glamor; and your steadfastness and your peril are your glory'. Tanner's insistence that he and Ann are giving up happiness in favour of familial responsibilities has little in common with this passage's tone of noble severity (which owes much to Shaw's beloved John Bunyan, who had also chronicled the journey of a pilgrim to the Heavenly City), but in his grandiloquent way Tanner is saying much the same thing. No less than Juan, he and Ann will give up happiness to 'live and work'; because their work is that of bettering society and breeding the future it is essential; but because it must be carried on in the world of fallible humanity, it is also laughable.

Don Juan's work is supposedly similar though conducted on an altogether higher plane. He is to ascend to heaven and by spending his 'eons in contemplation' will somehow assist in 'the work of helping Life in its struggle upward'. But there is, of course, a crucial difference in the nature of their efforts. People like Tanner and Ann really do write pamphlets and get married, but Juan's action is entirely metaphorical. Shaw is not only creating a set of imaginative circumstances in which he can expound his theory of Creative Evolution but he is dramatising in these symbolic terms a spiritual action that he has often dramatised before, that of withdrawal from human affairs, here ingeniously concealed (above all from himself) in the guise of a higher engagement in them.

The roots of this darker Shavian impulse undoubtedly extend into the area of familial and sexual entanglements that he deals with in so many plays. But there are also broader intellectual fears troubling Shaw's optimistic vision. For the notion that we can will an evolutionary ascent limited only by the achieving of the godhead depends on humanity's being essentially good, that is creative rather than destructive, and on the existence of some universal purpose that drives life onward. These assumptions, however, are precisely those questioned by the very Shavian Devil who presides over a Hell dominated by the love of music and the sexless flirtations that characterised aspects of Shaw's own life. Certainly it is Shaw's voice that sounds when the Devil expresses his contempt for 'machinery that a greedy dog could have invented if it had wanted money instead of food', for gentility as 'an excuse for consuming without producing', and for the populace that encourages military expenditures 'whilst the strongest Ministers dare not spend an extra penny in the pound against the poverty and pestilence through which they themselves daily walk'. Although Don Juan is allowed to contradict the Devil's contention that man is essentially a destroyer, that 'the power that governs the earth is not the power of Life but of Death' by arguing that man is not evil but only cowardly (till he is made valiant by some higher idea), the audience remembers the Devil's eloquence, by reason of length at least, rather than Juan's evasion. When the question of purpose arises just before Don Juan's departure it is once again the Devil who has the most trenchant phrase: 'You think because you have a purpose', he says to Juan, 'Nature must have one. You might as well expect it to have fingers and toes because you have them'. Instead of referring to the purpose of achieving godhead, already enunciated, Juan suggests the philosopher's brain, through which the Life Force comes to know its path, as the equivalent for Nature of physical organs. And when the Devil is unconvinced, arguing that in the service of the Life Force, one merely wastes the power of enjoyment, Juan replies that at least he escapes boredom, the state to which the hell of love and beauty had reduced him. On this ambiguous note, with the questions of purpose and of evil unresolved, Don Juan withdraws to his heaven of contemplation, leaving Ana, abruptly transformed from the conventional woman of the debate (Don Juan had fled the possessiveness of such women as Shaw had fled from Jenny Patterson's demands) to an embodiment of the creative principle demanding from the universe 'a father for the Superman!' But the universe has no answer, except perhaps for the sadly desperate breeding projects in Section X of *The Revolutionist's Handbook*, and the philosopher-amorist has been adroit enough to depart before his services could be called upon. John Tanner and Ann Whitefield must manage as best they can in the limited world of the human comedy.

John Bull's Other Island

When Shaw returned to the theatre with a new play, completed in the summer of 1904, that world of human comedy at once amusing and contemptible and that other world in which the elect among the damned could contemplate their distance from heaven were merged into what was for their creator a disturbing entity, the dramatic vision of his native country, Ireland. *John Bull's Other Island* was written at the request of W. B. Yeats for his Irish Literary Theatre, but the play made severe demands on the mechanical capacities of the Abbey Theatre and was not entirely congenial to Yeats' company; instead it was done by Granville-Barker at the Court despite Shaw's warning that the concluding conversation would 'stagger the very soul of Vedrenne [the cautious business manager] and send the audience away howling'.[3] In the event, it sent the English audience away laughing (the Englishman of the play is ultimately triumphant in love and commerce) and became a notable theatrical success. Today the play is difficult to stage (though it will work when done with care) because of its length, its loose structure, its dated politics, and its dubious view of the dubious subject of national character. (Indeed, Shaw's argument in the Preface that the Englishman 'is wholly at the mercy of his imagination, having no sense of reality to check it' is not even borne out by the play, in which Broadbent, for all his fatuousness, is perfectly well aware of what he must do to get elected to Parliament and to implement his land development scheme. The depiction of the small-mindedness of the Irish farmers does not distinguish them from any other peasantry, and one is left with the traditional characterisation of the Irish as clever dreamers – who 'can bear nothing real at all', as the play has it, again contradicting Shaw in the Preface, where he claims the Irishman 'has one eye always on things as they are'.) But despite its technical problems and the weakness of its claims to illuminate Anglo-Irish character and relations, *John Bull's Other Island* remains deeply appealing, for it is one of Shaw's most personal utterances.

As he had done in *Man and Superman*, Shaw brings on

stage characters who embody his own contradictory
impulses, to live in the world doing the necessary work of
bettering it and to withdraw from the world and its
coarseness to a realm of more exalted satisfactions. But
now he adds a third figure, the tormented exiled Irishman
Larry Doyle, who, like his creator, has left Ireland and
made his way to success in London. Poised on the
boundary between the ordinary world of facts and the
visionary world of dreams, he longs for some unity
between them. To his friend Broadbent, the hearty
Englishman who is at ease in his world, Doyle says, 'I wish
I could find a country to live in where the facts were not
brutal and the dreams not unreal'. In Doyle one recognises
that Shaw is evoking something of the character of his Don
Juan, shrinking from the demands of the world of the flesh
and yet equally unable to endure the illusions of the hell of
romance. Indeed Shaw's stage direction introducing
Doyle, which describes him as having '*cold grey eyes . . .
fastidious lips, critical brows*' and as being '*goodlooking
on the whole*' is an echo, evidently unconscious, of his
description of Don Juan as possessing in comparison with
Tanner a '*more critical, fastidious, handsome face, paler
and colder*'. And where Don Juan is '*without Tanner's
impetuous credulity and enthusiasm*' Doyle has a
'*suggestion of thinskinedness and dissatisfaction that
contracts strongly with Broadbent's eupeptic jollity*'.[4] But
for all his restless sensitivity, Doyle remains bound to the
mortal world; it is the unfrocked priest Peter Keegan who
recognises that world as hell and glimpses beyond it the
plains of heaven. Nor, though their 'gift of the gab' will no
doubt carry them to Parliament, is Tom Broadbent, the
Gladstonian liberal and capitalist entrepreneur, to be
entirely confounded with Jack Tanner, gentleman and
revolutionary.

Broadbent is, in fact, a more elusive figure than at first he seems. He begins as a man who is easily duped by a 'seedy swindler', as Doyle calls him, who has picked up his Irishness 'at the theatre or the music hall'; he sentimentalises to the swindler about the Irish as his 'warmhearted, impulsive countrymen' and answers Doyle's denunciation of the Irish imagination that evades coping with physical and moral squalor with fatuously anticlimactic earnestness: 'Never despair, Larry. There are great possibilities for Ireland. Home Rule will work wonders under English guidance'. The humour here is rich enough to accomplish a number of things: it ridicules Broadbent's chauvinism as the last phrase undercuts his initial assurance that there are 'great possibilities for Ireland'; simultaneously it justifies Doyle's desperation by suggesting that the Irish will accomplish nothing without 'English guidance' and yet sweeps that despair away in the laughter at Broadbent's triumphant foolishness.

The same mixture of success and ridicule attends Broadbent in his role as a lover. Although in Shaw's fantasy Nora Reilly, the sheltered Irish 'heiress', is really drawn to his more ascetic self, Larry Doyle, she is half unwillingly swept up by his fleshly incarnation, but not before Broadbent has been '*scared and much upset*' at finding himself attracted to Nora during their first interview, comically mothered by her when he is supposed to be drunk, and later reduced to impotent tearfulness:

BROADBENT: [*flushed and almost choking*] I dont want to be petted and blarneyed. [*With childish rage*] I love you. I want you for my wife. [*In despair*] I cant help your refusing. Im helpless: I can do nothing. You have no right to ruin my whole life. You – [*a hysterical convulsion stops him*].

Even though he bullies Nora, more or less, into accepting him and then sweeps her into his ludicrous, but no doubt successful political campaign, Broadbent experiences some of the 'childishness' that overcomes so many Shavian lovers when confronted by women. And finally Broadbent is no less ambiguous a figure in his economic than in his amorous activities. The doctrine of efficiency that he represents has the genuine virtue of being supra-national ('I shall collar this place', he says, 'not because I'm an Englishman and Haffigan and Co are Irishmen, but because theyre duffers, and I know my way about'), but his development scheme involves the ruthless displacement of the Roscullen villagers and the manipulating of a double bankruptcy to ruin the original investors and get the proposed hotel 'for a few shillings in the pound'. This is, of course, the plan that Shaw later attributes to Mangan in *Heartbreak House*; it is evidently the Shavian symbol for the commercial betrayal of moral values. Nevertheless, Broadbent's plan to 'make a Garden city of Roscullen' with 'a library, a Polytechnic (undenominational, of course) . . . perhaps an art school', however vulgar, is to be admired up to a point; it even hints at Perivale St Andrews, the garden city of Andrew Undershaft, the greater capitalist of Shaw's next play. In a moment during the final discussion with Keegan, Broadbent is even allowed to speak in the unmistakable Shavian-Carlylean voice:

BROADBENT: . . . But you know, something must be done.
KEEGAN: Yes: when we cease to do, we cease to live. Well, what shall we do?
BROADBENT: Why, what lies to our hand.

Despite his utter inability, half annoying and half

endearing, to understand the higher thought of either Keegan or Doyle, despite his crude ambitions and ruthlessness in business, Broadbent is doing what must be done: changing the world for the better. It is this that leads Doyle, for all his vastly superior sensitivity, to throw in his lot with Broadbent. Although Doyle has a quasi-socialist sense that those who have held the land should be called 'to a strict account for the use they made of it', he is so revolted by what he sees as the Irish infatuation with 'dreaming' and 'imagination' on the one hand and the mindless greed of the peasants who have succeeded the old landlords on the other, that he turns to Broadbent as the best available alternative. 'If we cant have men of honor own the land', he cries, 'lets have men of ability. If we cant have men with ability, let us at least have men with capital'. Nevertheless, as a presence in the play, Doyle hovers tormentedly between the visionary world of Keegan and the practical one of Broadbent. 'Life's too earthly for him:' Broadbent says of Doyle, 'he doesn't really care for anything or anybody'. Although he is said to prefer women 'solid and bouncing', like Don Juan, for whom even imaginative life was too earthly, he escapes the lures of the feminine, but only for a state of permanent discontent. 'I want you;' he tells Nora after they have broken off, 'and I quarrel with you and have to go on wanting you'. Similarly he must go on longing futilely for an Ireland where the people will live by their higher capacities ('We're like the Jews: the Almighty gave us brains, and bid us farm them and leave the clay and the worms alone') and where 'the people is the Church and the Church the people'.

Not Doyle, however, but Peter Keegan truly commits himself to this vision of mystic unity. Described in his introductory stage direction as having '*the face of a young saint, yet with white hair'*, he stares into the sunset as if he could *'by mere intensity of gaze . . . see into the streets of heaven'*. His longing for heaven is only intensified by his recognition of the world as hell – not Don Juan's hell of vapid romance but an altogether cruder one epitomised in Barney Doran's story of the automobile and the pig. For the villagers who hear Doran tell it, the tale of the pig Broadbent was attempting to deliver in his motor car, which leaped into the driver's seat and, in effect, drove wildly through the town causing damage and eventually its own death, is a farcical diversion: for Keegan this rejoicing at 'danger, destruction, torment' is monstrous. Moved by a Shavian sense of the sacred unity of life, he tells Doran, with uncomprehended irony, to continue regaling the company with the details of the animal's death: 'Go on, Barney: the last drops of joy are not squeezed from the story yet. Tell us again how our brother was torn asunder'. And as Doran blunders coarsely on, Keegan murmurs '[*with intense emphasis*] It is hell: it is hell. Nowhere else could such a scene be a burst of happiness for the people'. Later he amplifies his vision of the world as 'a place of torment and penance' that Broadbent's efforts at improvement will only make into a 'clean and orderly' prison. That Keegan's is a Shavian vision becomes even clearer when, in the 'transcendental conversation', as Shaw called it[5], near the end of the play, he tells Broadbent that the ass (Broadbent himself in Keegan's not unkind metaphor), 'the most efficient of beasts, matter-of-fact, hardy, friendly', nevertheless 'wastes all his virtues – his efficiency as you call it – in doing the will of his greedy masters instead of doing the will of heaven that is in himself'. The divine will that is part of the self is always, for Shaw, the will of the Life Force, ultimately to transcend human limitations and create the heaven which Keegan says that in his madness he envisions:

> In my dreams it is a country where the State is the Church and the Church the people: three in one and one in three. It is a commonwealth in which work is play and play is life: three in one and one in three. It is a temple in which the priest is the worshipper and the worshipper the worshipped: three in one and one in three. It is a godhead in which all life is human and all humanity divine: three in one and one in three. It is, in short, the dream of a madman.

It is, of course, also Shaw's dream of the Heavenly City, the visionary place to which the Shavian saints so often withdraw. Here, as Keegan says, there is an absolute unity between the religious and secular lives of the citizens, whose work is the ecstasy of raising life to a higher level, who as both priests and congregants worship the Life Force within themselves and recognise it as one with the vital impulse of the universe. As Keegan '*goes away across the hill*' to his world of contemplation near the Round Tower and Broadbent calls on Doyle to help him choose the site for their hotel, these figures, embodying equally insistent Shavian demands, pursue their irreconcilable courses.

Major Barbara

While he was working on *John Bull's Other Island*, Shaw took a few days to dash off *How He Lied to Her Husband*, a one-act whimsy for Arnold Daly, who needed a curtain-raiser for *The Man of Destiny*. Taking up the familiar *Candida* material of the husband, wife, and youthful poet-lover, he turned it to farce by making the husband so vain of his wife's charms that he insists on advertising the poet's liaison with her, even on publishing his love poems. In writing his next play, this time a major effort, Shaw again drew upon his own work, turning to a pattern he had used earlier, but now instead of trivialising it, he vastly enriched and expanded it, producing one of the masterpieces of his career and indeed of the modern drama. Shaw himself seems at some point to have recognised the connection between *Major Barbara* (completed in the summer of 1905) and its progenitor, for he later suggested to his biographer Archibald Henderson that 'Perhaps a more suitable title for this play, save for the fact of repetition, would have been *Andrew Undershaft's Profession*'.[6] Despite the extraordinary differences in temperament between the coarsely passionate brothel keeper of *Mrs Warren's Profession* and the mysterious munitions maker of the greater play, they stand in close relationship to each other. Each is a 'wicked' parent who, though impoverished in youth, has become successful and provided richly for a daughter while remaining largely or entirely absent during her childhood. Upon re-entering the life of the now adult, high-minded daughter, the parent convinces her that his supposedly evil career was, under the circumstances, a necessary, even moral one providing self-respect for the parent and a decent life for the child. In a crucial confrontation about halfway through the play the parent is able to demonstrate the weakness of the child's moral position and reveal to her much about the economic evils of society. These parents envisage the daughters as in some way carrying on their values, but in each case the daughter, in the more difficult second half of the play, reasserts her own values and comes to personal terms with the parent. When we recall that *Mrs Warren's Profession* is itself a reworking of *Widower's Houses*, we are able to recognise in Sartorius – the great slum landlord, the revealer of brutal economic truths, the self-made man of power who draws his daughter's fiancé into his dubious enterprises – the ultimate Shavian source of Andrew Undershaft.

But the 'Mammoth Millionaire' of *Major Barbara* is no mere exploiter of decaying real estate; a diabolic proto-Superman with an admixture of Caesar's ingratiating humour, he presides beneficently over a workers' paradise even as he deals in death and destruction. From such contradictory elements in Undershaft's character and career as well as from his ambiguous relationship with his daughter and her fiancé stem many of the play's difficulties and much of its richness. Even before Undershaft appears in the play, his elusive nature is prefigured in the name of his firm: Undershaft and Lazarus. That Lazarus is, as we learn in the last act, 'a gentle romantic Jew who cares for nothing but string quartets and stalls at fashionble theatres' does not alter the fact that his name suggests both the traditional Jewish financier and the idea of resurrection. But before Undershaft can raise his daughter to a new life, if that is indeed what he does (he is also, perhaps, engaged in the greater task of raising society to a higher level), he must make her die to her old one. As it was in *Mrs Warren's Profession*, the assertion of economic truth is also a demonstration of parental power, social and personal elements being characteristically intertwined in Shaw's drama.

Many of the difficulties of *Major Barbara* are associated with these personal elements whereas, especially in the earlier part of the play, the economic argument is made with dramatic force and intellectual lucidity. When Undershaft arrives at his wife's home, he is at once humanised by the farcical byplay of the misunderstood introductions (suitably, the primary joke is Undershaft's inability to recognise Stephen, whose values are in exact opposition to his own, as his son) and made intriguing by his unexpected interest in religion. As the act draws to a close, he and Barbara exchange the mutual challenges to visit each other's establishments – in effect, to test the power of Barbara's religion against that of Undershaft's money – that are the motive force of the play. The victory of Undershaft is prefigured in the greater symbolic weight of his reply when he responds to Barbara after asking where he can find her shelter:

> BARBARA: In West Ham. At the sign of the cross. Ask anybody in Canning Town. Where are your works?
> UNDERSHAFT: In Perivale St Andrews. At the sign of the sword. Ask anybody in Europe.

The scheme of the play is clearly that Barbara's illusions are to be destroyed when her father visits the shelter and Undershaft's truth to be established when his daughter visits the factory. The latter aim is only partially realised, but the first is fully achieved.

Undershaft's immediate economic message has two parts: that the Salvation Army and indeed all charities depend upon donations from the rich and that they serve the interests of the rich by keeping the poor docile. In Act II, as brilliant and masterful a scene as anything Shaw ever wrote, the latter point is made at once by Snobby Price (who achieves a comic triumph over the restraints of the Salvation Army and indeed over the moral judgement of the audience by the creative enthusiasm with which he throws himself into his role as a reformed sinner). To Rummy Mitchens' complaint that it is not right for the army to deny women the opportunity to make a show of their supposed sins, Snobby replies with a shrewdly ironic paradox: 'Right! Do you spose the Army'd be allowed if it went and did right? Not much. It combs our air and makes us good little blokes to be robbed and put upon'. ('It draws their teeth', Undershaft adds later, speaking of the Army and the poor.) When near the end of the act Mrs Baines displays Snobby as a 'good little bloke', she is only confirming publicly what he has already revealed.

Undershaft himself, however, makes the demonstration of his primary point, that 'all religious organizations exist by selling themselves to the rich'. Barbara shall know, he determines, that anyone who wishes to alleviate hardship must accept the tainted wealth offered by Bodger and himself, wealth deriving from 'Drunkenness and Murder' as Barbara in her anguish says (from competitive capitalism that inevitably trades in poverty and its consequences as Shaw would say). The demonstration is quite schematic although, immersed in the rich texture of the act, it does not immediately seem so. In a street meeting highlighted by Snobby's recital of his supposed past wickednesses, Barbara has collected four shillings and tenpence ('Oh Snobby', she says mischievously, 'if you had given your poor mother just one more kick, we should have got the whole five shillings'). When Undershaft offers to contribute the missing two pence, 'the millionaire's mite, eh?' Barbara refuses: 'You cant buy your Salvation here for twopence: you must work it out'. She takes the same line, that 'the Army is not to be bought' a little later when Bill Walker tries to escape the claim of his conscience by offering the Army a pound. Angered by her refusal, he taunts Barbara by suggesting that only 'a anderd pahnd' will do for 'a earl's grendorter'. Now Undershaft offers ninety-nine pounds to make up the hundred, but Barbara still refuses, comparing her father's offer with that made to the archetypal betrayer: 'Oh, youre too extravagant, papa. Bill offers twenty pieces of silver. All you need offer is the other ten'. But when her father's offer of five thousand pounds is gratefully accepted by the Army and she understands it must be, Barbara is desolated by the realisation that Bill's taunting question, 'Wot prawce Sevlytion nah?' has a quite specific answer.

Undershaft's truth and Barbara's despair are both dramatically convincing because they have the cumulative weight of the whole act behind them, but in the looser, more discursive Act III the arguments must depend more on the force of Shaw's rhetoric.[7] At first, it works well enough. In his interview with Stephen, Undershaft is able to suggest the unscrupulous and wide-ranging power of capitalist enterprise (somewhat in the manner of George Croft's discoursing to Vivie and expanding the specific point – in that case the economics of prostitution – driven home there as here at the end of Act II) and his contempt for the politics and government that Stephen so admires:

UNDERSHAFT: [*with a touch of brutality*] The government of your country! *I* am the government of your country: I, and Lazarus. Do you suppose that you and half a dozen amateurs like you, sitting in a row in that foolish gabble shop, can govern Undershaft and Lazarus? No, my friend: you will do what pays us. You will make war when it suits us, and keep peace when it doesnt. You will find out that trade requires certain measures when we have decided on those measures. . . . And in return you shall have the support and applause of my newspapers, and the delight of imagining that you are a great statesman.

That Undershaft the munitions maker should at this point

openly confirm the classic socialist complaint against capitalist power is less improbable than it seems, given his background. Sufficiently annoyed at Stephen here to be indiscreet, he is the person in the play most powerfully conscious of the terrible result of unrestrained industrial competition, of what he chooses to call the 'crime' of poverty. (Shaw may owe this richly evocative metaphor, suggesting that poverty is a pathological social phenomenon no more to be tolerated than any curable condition, to Samuel Butler, whom he extolls in the *Major Barbara* preface, and whose *Erewhon* offers readers the more elusive metaphor of the 'crime' of illness.) When, during their confrontation at Perivale, Cusins, astonished at this use of the terms, asks if poverty is a crime, Undershaft responds with one of Shaw's most penetrating social utterances:

> The worst of crimes. All other crimes are virtues beside it: all other dishonours are chivalry itself by comparison. Poverty blights whole cities; spreads horrible pestilences; strikes dead the very souls of all who come within sight, sound or smell of it. What you call crime is nothing . . . there are not fifty genuine professional criminals in London. But there are millions of poor people, abject people, dirty people, ill fed, ill clothed people. They poison us morally and physically: they kill the happiness of society: they force us to do away with our own liberties and to organize unnatural cruelties for fear they should rise against us and drag us down into their abyss. Only fools fear crime: we all fear poverty.

The profound social empathy that Undershaft demonstrates here takes us far from the figure of the ruthless, if mysterious entrepreneur whom we met in the earlier acts. But a few moments later even this quality is replaced by something very like revolutionary fervour. 'Poverty and slavery', he says, 'have stood up for centuries to your leading articles: they will not stand up to my machine guns. Dont preach at them: dont reason with them. Kill them'. The rhetorical force of its ever tightening phrases carries this speech along, but its meaning is not quite clear for, though the machine guns are real, their proposed targets are abstractions. However, Undershaft does at times seem to mean literal shooting. Killing, he tells Barbara, is 'the only lever strong enough to overturn a social system'. 'When you vote', he goes on to assure Cusins, 'you only change the names in the cabinet. When you shoot, you pull down governments, inaugurate new epochs, abolish old orders and set up new'. Pressing home his point, he demands, 'Is that historically true, Mr Learned Man, or is it not?' and Cusins grants his claim. 'Come and make explosives with me', Undershaft cries exultantly. 'Whatever can blow men up can blow society up'.

If this appeal is taken literally, Undershaft seems to envision Perivale as a sort of revolutionary armoury, at the gates of which he and Cusins will one day stand passing out weapons to an aroused proletariat that will initiate an era of anarchist violence. The image would be grotesque and the circumstances incredible even if one were unacquainted with Shaw's commitment to Fabian gradualism and his deep belief that the police powers of the state could easily deal with any insurrection. (The Shaw who writes in the Sane Conclusions section of the Preface to *Major Barbara*, 'I am, and have always been, and shall now always be, a revolutionary writer' has, as the *now* of this phrase so sadly confirms, come to accept the long continuation of an unjust society and his consequent alienation from it.) Thus Undershaft, despite the actuality of his weapons, must be understood at the end of the play to be speaking metaphorically (one can literally blow men up but not society); he is clearly not doing so at the beginning, however. Enthusiastic about the efficiency of his weapons, he appears at first a diabolical figure, a capitalist monster with an amiable exterior; gradually he is revealed as a man of high social conscience, and finally transformed into a symbol of socialist and revolutionary aspiration. Considering this instability in the treatment of Undershaft, what is surprising is not that there are problems in Act III as the aesthetic ground shifts beneath one but that the character as a dramatic presence remains constant and evocative throughout.

Part of the reason for Undershaft's viability is that he is richly involved with all the themes of the play. He opposes Barbara on religious as well as economic grounds, and here too difficulties arise as the play develops. In Act I, his concern for religion appears in his assurance that he does not find it 'an unpleasant subject', that it is in fact 'the only one that capable people really care for'. This assurance is less surprising than it might be if he had not already asserted an opposition to the Christianity 'which enjoins you to resist not evil', and goes on to say, 'My morality – my religion – must have a place for cannons and torpedoes in it'. This cryptic assertion is not elucidated by his assurance to Barbara, in Act II, that he is 'a confirmed mystic' and his response to her query as to his religion: 'Well, my dear, I am a Millionaire. That is my religion'. However, when he explains to Cusins that in this creed salvation depends upon 'Money and Gunpowder', that is to say 'money enough for a decent life and power enough to be your own master', it becomes clear that what has appeared to be a religion of riches and destruction is in fact a 'faith' in the necessity for social progress. It might seem that Shaw was simply decorating a secular concept with theological language, but to the Creative Evolutionist the movement towards a higher level of social development is only an aspect of the Life Force's struggle to attain a superior stage of spiritual organisation. In resolving that Barbara shall preach his 'gospel' of 'money and gunpowder; freedom and power; command of life and command of death', Undershaft reveals himself as an agent of the Force (as he puts it, 'a will of which I am a part') that is finally to free man from his mortal, physical self.

This complex Shavian mingling of secular purpose and religious aspiration is also characteristic of Barbara. One finds out little about Barbara's religion in Act I except that she is good-humoured and practical in her piety. Strangely enough, one finds out little more in Act II when she is actually seen attempting a conversion, for her appeals to Bill Walker, though she mentions in passing 'Somebody or something that wants to make a man of you', are directed to whatever innate conscience he may have ('a man with a heart wouldnt have bashed poor little Jenny's face, would he?'), and when she finally asks him to come with the Army to 'brave manhood on earth and eternal glory in heaven', the final phrase seems an irrelevant intrusion. But even more problematic than Barbara's demonstration of faith in the middle of the act is her loss of it at the end. After all, Undershaft has demonstrated nothing about the Salvation Army except that as a charitable institution it is, like others, dependent on donations from the wealthy. Whatever his action has revealed about the moral position of the Army, it has no bearing on the existence or non-existence of a divine being, yet for Barbara that revelation appears to have resulted in an absolute loss of faith. She

163

says that she may 'never pray again' and in her desolation even exclaims with Christ 'My God: why has thou forsaken me?' In the last act she is even more explicit in speaking to her father of her sense of loss: 'I was safe with an infinite wisdom watching me, an army marching to Salvation with me; and in a moment, at a stroke of your pen in a check book, I stood alone; and the heavens were empty'.

Barbara's desolation here is the more curious in that she had already been revivified by her father's suggestion that she had left an indelible moral 'mark' on Bill Walker. 'Oh, you are right:' she exclaims, 'he can never be lost now: where was my faith?' Whether her faith has in fact been found or lost, Barbara is moved by her father's assertion that he is part of a greater will ('Father! Do you know what you are saying; or are you laying a snare for my soul?') and at the end of the play has perhaps responded to Undershaft's encouraging advice: 'If your old religion broke down yesterday, get a newer and a better one for tomorrow'. Soon after, he invites Barbara to try her hand as a saver of souls on his men: 'their souls are hungry because their bodies are full'. Nothing that Undershaft has said about Perivale, which despite its comfort is a hierarchy of snobbery and authoritarianism, suggests that this is so, but Barbara finally declares that she is drawn to 'all human souls to be saved' there; 'Major Barbara will die with the colors . . . Glory Hallelujah!' The rhetoric of this passage may carry it in the theatre, but it is difficult to imagine Barbara setting out to establish a unit of the Salvation Army in Perivale, especially as Undershaft has mentioned that his men are, conventionally at least, religious already.

However, a passage immediately preceding this one suggests that the banner to which Barbara has rallied may be that of a quite different religion. Speaking to Cusins, she announces her new resolve:

> My father shall never throw it in my teeth again that my converts were bribed with bread [*She is transfigured*]. I have got rid of the bribe of bread. I have got rid of the bribe of heaven. Let God's work be done for its own sake: the work he had to create us to do because it cannot be done except by living men and women. When I die, let him be in my debt, not I in his; and let me forgive him as becomes a woman of my rank.

In the instant of transfiguration Barbara seems to have grasped the essence of a religion that dispenses with the idea of personal survival in an afterlife, one in which the divine will is not omnipotent and must achieve its ends through the creatures that it has evolved for this purpose. No Shavian could fail to recognise the suggestion of Creative Evolution here. Theologically, in fact, the Salvation Army has never really been part of this play. Shaw has moved Barbara from a pseudo-evangelical enthusiasm for moral regeneration through a dubious loss of faith to a religious commitment that he thought suitable for certain aspects of Perivale, which is, if not a 'heavenly city' as Cusins calls it, at least a city of the future.

But the last phrases of Barbara's speech – those concerning debt and forgiveness – are harder to gloss, for they do not refer to Creative Evolution and perhaps not even ultimately to religious belief in general. *Major Barbara*, after all, is a play about more than money and religion, and its personages are more than financiers and believers: they are also parents and children and lovers. Before trying to elucidate Barbara's cryptic words, it will be well to consider how the characters function in these roles. The first people we meet in the play are mother and son; the scene in which they appear establishes not only the background of the Undershaft inheritance but the nature of child-parent relationships in Lady Britomart's household.[8] Although she is lively, good-humoured, and high-spirited, Lady Britomart is in relation to her children possessive and domineering. The sweetness of Shaw's comedy defuses but does not disguise this quality as Lady Britomart's earnest boast of political liberalism becomes an outrageous assertion of parental tyranny: 'And my family, thank Heaven, is not a pig-headed Tory one. We are Whigs, and believe in liberty. Let snobbish people say what they please: Barbara shall marry, not the man they like, but the man *I* like'. With a combination of maternal affection and ruthless ingenuity she bullies Stephen into assenting to her schemes, leaving him finally '*outwitted and overwhelmed*'. (Her persistent denunciations of the endearingly vapid Charles Lomax are transpositions of the same material into a farcical key.) But Stephen revenges himself in Act III by haughtily excluding his mother from his talk with Undershaft about his future, which, he says with crude masculine vanity, 'had better take place with my father, as between one man and another'. Lady Britomart is profoundly wounded, and they end the scene in a state of icy estrangement.

Between these two scenes comes Act II with its focus on the Salvation Army's economic vulnerability. Nevertheless, the conflict between the demanding parent and the rebellious child is continued, but now in an altered form. Lady Britomart has noticed Barbara's 'propensity to have her own way and order people about' but, innocently unaware that these are her own tendencies, adds with unconscious irony, 'I'm sure I dont know where she picked it up'. And at one point in Act II Shaw describes

Barbara as being '*indignant, in her mother's manner*', but Barbara's maternal bullying takes the more subtle form of a supposedly religious appeal. However, as we have noted, the Bill Walker episode has in actuality little to do with religion, whereas it has much to do with demands for moral reform and particularly with demands that feminine figures be respected. Bill's response to Barbara's 'neggin and provowkin' is the quintessential child's response to maternal demands – tears. Shaw describes him as being '*to his great shame and terror, in danger of crying*' and at another point as '*almost crying*' and exclaiming desperately, 'Ow, will you lea me alown?' Bill is too much intimidated by Barbara's social rank to do more than advise Cusins to 'stop er jawr', but with other women he is, like Stephen, prepared to be brutal, but in an exclusively physical way. Having come to the shelter to revenge himself on his girl, he plans to 'brike her jawr' and succeeds in striking both Jenny and Rummy. It is, of course, Snobby Price who, in his fantasy life, beats his mother (though in reality she used to beat him), and even the kindly Peter Shirley has attended a coroner's inquest on his daughter.

This diffused anti-feminism touches even Cusins who agrees whimsically with Bill's warning that if he marries Barbara, he will die before his time, 'wore aht'. 'Yes, my dear', Cusins tells her, 'it's very wearing to be in love with you. If it lasts, I quite think I shall die young'. Though Cusins is playful here, he will seriously assent to Barbara's reminder that he is not the centre of her life:

BARBARA: . . . There are larger loves and diviner dreams than the fireside ones. You know that, dont you?

CUSINS: Yes: that is our understanding.

The notion that there are both limitations and perils in relations with women is extended even to the remote and powerful Undershaft, whose confession that he has fallen in love with Barbara 'with a father's love', provokes Cusins' warning that 'A father's love for a grown-up daughter is the most dangerous of all infatuations'. Barbara does not present the sort of threats posed by the young Queen of Egypt, but Cusins' admonition is curiously reminiscent of a previous suggestion that Cleopatra would be 'the most dangerous of all Caesar's conquests'.

The demands that Barbara makes of Undershaft involve not worldly power but human affection (though Shaw understood that these phenomena are never entirely separable). The same demands are, in fact, made by Cusins, but he and Barbara react differently to Undershaft's response. Coping with the moral difficulties posed by Undershaft's invitation, Cusins raises the question of universal love but then narrows it to one instance: 'May I not even love my father-in-law?' The nascent Superman rejects this appeal to emotions: 'Who wants your love, man? . . . I will have your due heed and respect, or I will kill you. But your love! Damn your impertinence!' However, Cusins who is shortly to join Undershaft in doing the world's work, amiably teases the surrogate father whom he has called Machiavelli: '[*grinning*] I may not be able to control my affections, Mac'. A moment later Barbara puts the same query to Undershaft but in a more anguished tone and with a wider application: 'Father: do you love nobody?' Undershaft seems to have taken Cusins' warning to heart, for despite his protestations of Act II, he answers Barbara not with fatherly affection but with something between a high-sounding evasion and a lesson in exalted morality: 'I love my best friend [who is] My bravest enemy. That is the man who keeps me up to the mark'. For Barbara this rejection must be particularly painful since she has set out not only, like her mother, to extend her emotional authority but, like her father, to be a revealer of truth to the world. But Dionysis-Undershaft brooks no rivals: even in succession there is authority: 'I shall hand on my torch to my daughter. She shall make my converts and preach my gospel—'. Barbara is thus a peculiarly ambiguous figure: she is herself an extension of feminine and parental power, but she is also the child-victim of parental rejection and parental will. Whatever Shaw's mixed feelings about feminine demands, he had been a rejected child and had made himself into the parental advice-giver to the world; he is thus deeply sympathetic to Barbara in both these incarnations and at the conclusion of the play allows her the expression of impulses appropriate to each.

The parental stance takes a form familiar from other Shavian works, most notably the passage in *Man and Superman* where Don Juan withdraws himself from human concerns and departs for a heaven of contemplation. To Cusins – who like Tanner is committed to work, perhaps even to revolution – Barbara says in a moment of annoyance, 'Oh, if only I could get away from you and from father and from it all! if I could have the wings of a dove and fly away to heaven!' When Cusins, aggrieved, exclaims, 'And leave me!' Barbara responds with maternal disdain, 'Yes, you, and all the other naughty mischievous children of men'. But more moving is the expression of filial pain, that found in the final sentence of the speech quoted earlier: 'When I die, let him be in my debt, not I in his; and let me forgive him as becomes a woman of my rank'. It is addressed to the ultimate Father, but the personal note is unmistakable. It is the voice of one who has determined to reverse the traditional roles of child and parent, to stand free of debt, to be the one who forgives (what unspeakable parental crime we do not know, but Undershaft's refusal to admit his love can hardly be irrelevant), to insist on one's rank, which is to say on the separateness of one's self. But Shaw is neither daring nor cruel enough to end his play on this note. Barbara becomes affectionately maternal, addressing Cusins as her 'dear little Dolly boy' and then childishly submissive, appealing to her mother to choose a house for her in the village; Shaw leaves only a hint of her secret desire to withdraw in Cusins' oddly evocative description of her happiness: 'She has gone right up into the skies'.

The Doctor's Dilemma

When Shaw returned to the stage in November of 1906 with a new play for Granville-Barker, he allowed it to end with the heroine rejecting the love of a paternal figure. (The note of utter alienation on which it concludes is perhaps a better justification of its subtitle, 'A Tragedy' than the existence, or even the death, of what its hero describes as 'the most tragic thing in the world', 'a man of genius who is not also a man of honor'.) But this harsh echo of a motif from *Major Barbara* and the ostensible appearance (developed at length in the Preface but only alluded to in the play) of an equivalent social theme (the limitations of private medicine paralleling those of private charity in *Major Barbara*) is deceptive, for the allegiance of *The Doctor's Dilemma* is not to its immediate predecessor but to an earlier Shavian work, *Candida*. Once again Shaw turns to the classic domestic triangle of the wife, the husband, and the would-be lover, the familiar resonances of the situation emphasised by the wife's being named Jennifer, the Cornish equivalent, as she points out, of Guinevere. However, she is characteristically for Shaw less a seductress than a maternal figure, but the essential variation on the theme lies in her being married to Lancelot (she calls him a King of Men in her idealising biography, but he is a far from perfect knight), leaving Arthur, in this case Sir Colenso Ridgeon, hampered by age and dignity, to play the ungrateful role of the guilty lover.

This familiar material lies somewhat obscured beneath a medical melodrama in which Ridgeon's 'dilemma' is that he must choose between applying his tuberculosis cure to his virtuous friend Dr Blenkinsop or to Jennifer's husband, the morally unscrupulous but artistically talented Dubedat.[9] (His name suggests both his dubious nature and his 'gift' as a painter). Running concurrently with the central action, and further blurring the focus on it, is what one might call a satiric medical farce in which, after some introductory conversational flourishes on the peculiarities of medical practice, the audience is offered two endearing caricatures in the tradition of Molière and Dickens: Cutler Walpole, obsessed with cutting out the 'nuciform sac' to avoid 'blood poisoning', and the splendidly fatuous Sir Ralph Bloomfield Bonnington who blunders amiably through the play labouring under the delusion, literally fatal, that any sort of 'really stiff anti-toxin' will sufficiently 'stimulate the phagocytes' to cure any disease. The result of their presence – and especially of Sir Ralph's bumbling – is not only to help salvage an otherwise dangerously sentimental death scene, for Shaw with a sure and daring sense of their effect in performance keeps them as funny here as elsewhere, but by association to undermine our sense of the worth and dignity of Ridgeon's work, even though his powers as a physician are, in the context of the play, taken seriously.

But the major assault on Ridgeon and his colleagues is mounted by Dubedat who, though like Marchbanks physically frail, is also bold in defending his values against the weight of quasi-paternal disapproval. When Dubedat announces that he is a 'disciple of Bernard Shaw' and justifies his self-indulgences with regard to money and women as a striving after what he supposes is the amoral ideal of the Superman, Shaw is consciously teasing himself and his public's misunderstandings, but he is also, no doubt unconsciously, affirming his identification with the rebellious child who disputes not only the paternal claim to moral and intellectual authority but the possession of the maternal figure as well. For Jennifer is, like Candida, the dream mother become young and beautiful, whose devotion to her surrogate son is boundless; she herself says of Dubedat, 'He came to me like a child . . . just like a boy . . . I gave him myself and all that I had that he might grow to his full height . . .'. And despite all the differences between these two plays, the final result of this relationship is almost precisely the same. As Marchbanks goes out 'into the night', Tristan's holy night of death, so Dubedat affirms his superiority in uttering his creed and leaves the world (like Don Juan, for a higher one: 'I'm in heaven', Dubedat says, 'immortal in the heart of my beautiful Jennifer') since the incest fantasy can hardly be long maintained in it.[10] Moreover, in this altogether bleaker play the ostensible happiness of the parental figures can be dispensed with and the dead child granted his secret wish: Ridgeon's revelation of his interest in Jennifer is greeted with disdain and implacable hostility. It was six years before Shaw's full powers as a playwright flowered again, and then it was in a play that ended in the same circumstances, a grinding disagreement frustrating the romance of an older man and a younger woman. Before *Pygmalion*, however, Shaw produced an intriguing body of work, one best considered in larger groupings.

Disquisitory Plays on Family and Religion

Although Shaw used the term 'disquisitory play' only for *Getting Married*, the first of this 'group', it may be fairly applied to most of them since they tend to become extended discourses presenting rather than embodying Shavian ideas; indeed, some of them seem almost to be appendages to lengthy prefaces, not always on the same subjects as the plays themselves. Of these plays, moreover, only *Misalliance* and *Androcles and the Lion* have sufficient theatrical allure (which is perhaps to say that only these become self-sustaining, metaphoric visions of life) to be part of the regularly performed Shavian repertory, and even their positions are marginal. Since this body of work focuses essentially on two topics, family relations and religion, it will be helpful to break strict chronology and look, briefly, at them in thematic terms.

In *Getting Married* (1906) a group of supremely loquacious figures of Shavian fantasy (many embodiments of attitudes or concepts ranging from British snobbery to Pauline Christianity) discourse at length on the ultimate familial themes: marriage and divorce. Although the characters all have a degree of quirky theatrical vitality, they finally remain voices rather than becoming dramatic entities; and thus the positions they exemplify or the ideas they advocate, often restated from the Preface, however shrewdly prescient (e.g. that a woman has a right to be paid for her household labour), tend to remain somewhat disembodied. As a result, the Shavian argument that divorce should be cheaply available on the simple request of either party is less dramatically evocative than the play's one extraordinary characterisation, that of the tormented prophetess Mrs George, an embodiment of the Life Force as Eternal Feminine, who in her inspired musings offers sexual ecstacy as creative transcendence and disdains the common demands of domesticity but who in her life puts the interests of her commonplace husband before those of her comparatively youthful pursuer, St John Hotchkiss (replicating the archetypical *Candida* situation), to whom Shaw has given his own significant childhood nickname of Sonny.

The intrusion of a remarkable woman upon an eccentric family occurring well on in the play) is also the most striking event of *Misalliance* (1909), but Lina Szczepanowska, though like Mrs George an emblem of sexual independence and feminine power, works by physical rather than spiritual means. In her grand oration she offers no vision of the Life Force but rather an extended comic denunciation of the position of women in a bourgeois household. The ostensible subject of the play, however, would seem to be the relations between parents and children (that is certainly the primary subject of the Preface; the play remains notably unfocused). But though it is discussed shrewdly by Tarleton and Summerhays, the two paternal figures (the discussion stops short of exploring Shaw's startling comment in the Preface: 'Until the family as we know it ceases to exist, nobody will dare to analyse parental affection . . .), and illustrated by their inability to control their obstreperous children, it is embodied in a to some degree theatrical action as the fathers become or reveal that they have been rivals for the younger women whom their sons are also pursuing. But in the world of Shavian comedy not only the fathers but the sons are summarily rejected by the play's vitally ruthless women in favour of freedom or a more sexually appetising alternative ('Papa:' says Hypatia, 'buy the brute for me'). A despair not dissimilar to Tarleton's is evinced by the self-consciously old fashioned Count O'Dowda of the 'potboiler' (Shaw's term) *Fanny's First Play* (1911) who is shocked by his rebellious daughter's 'first play', a play that is itself about rebellious children, though it ends whimsically with everyone suited and the heroine planning to be married to a comic butler who reveals himself as the brother of a Duke.

A rebellious child, one rebelling against the greatest Father, is also the central character of Shaw's 'Sermon in Crude Melodrama', *The Shewing-up of Blanco Posnet* (1909), whose scapegrace hero with his rejection of conventional piety reminds one of Dick Dudgeon, the main figure of Shaw's other melodrama with an American setting. (The West is peculiarly unconvincing in *Blanco Posnet*, but the picture is probably no further from the truth than the myths of American popular culture.) Like Dudgeon, Blanco sacrifices himself when confronted with a moral crisis and is tried, with his life at stake, as a result. In a moment of revelation after his last-minute rescue, he is vouchsafed an illumination – of the Shavian solution to the problem of evil, or at least of such horrors as the croup that has killed an innocent baby:

> What about the croup? It was early days when He made the croup, I guess. It was the best He could think of then; but when it turned out wrong on His hands He made you and me to fight the croup for Him. . . . He wouldnt have made us at all if He could have done His work without us.

The point here is not only that evil is explained as a mistake of the Life Force in its blundering progress, but that a family myth is posited in which a father who is incompetent, as the elder Shaw was incompetent, is in effect replaced by a gifted offspring whose skill is necessary if the world is to be saved.

The charming *Androcles and the Lion* (1912), the other religious play of this period, is less explicit intellectually than *Blanco Posnet* but much more attractive theatrically, being the least 'disquisitory' of these plays. It also contains an echo of *The Devil's Disciple* in the figure of Ferrovius who like Anthony Anderson finds his true vocation as a fighter in the moment of trial. (In the romance between the Christian maiden and the Roman soldier it also echoes Wilson Barrett's *The Sign of the Cross*, which Shaw had reviewed during his stint as a drama critic.)[11] Ultimately Androcles is not only about faith in an inner force that transcends Christian 'dreams and stories' but also about rebellion, in Lavinia's stubborn assertion of her beliefs, and even about Fabian gradualism in its playful assurance that the revolutionist (religious or other) of one age can evolve into the respectable citizen of the next.

The Later Group

Pygmalion

As Shaw had drawn upon a recollection of the nineties for *Androcles*, so he did for his next play, one of his richest, most theatrically vital creations, *Pygmalion*, which he completed in June of 1912. Writing to Ellen Terry on 8 September 1897, he had told her that he had conceived of a play for Forbes Robertson and Mrs Patrick Campbell 'in which he shall be a West End gentleman and she an East End dona in an apron and three orange and red ostrich feathers'. The persistence of Shaw's vision over the fifteen years that separate the letter and the play is testified to by the survival, substantially intact, of these details of costume; Shaw specifies a '*coarse apron*' for Eliza in Act I and '*a hat with three ostrich feathers, orange, sky-blue, and red*' in Act II. That Shaw gave the role of the eighteen-year-old flower girl to Mrs Pat, still beautiful but at forty-eight clearly a mature woman, is further testimony to that persistence; that she made a great success of it is proof of her talent and charm as well as of his shrewd judgement of actors.

Herbert Beerbohm Tree, who created the role of Higgins, was a more problematic figure. Though entirely amiable, Tree was according to Shaw so disorganised and obstructive (Shaw was the producer, but it was Tree's theatre) that twice Shaw threw up his hands in despair and deserted the rehearsals, only to be lured back by the other actors. Shaw insisted that Tree had 'no conception' of the 'Miltonic professor of phonetics' and wrote of his leading actor, 'when he resigned himself to his unnatural task, he set to work to make this disagreeable and incredible person sympathetic in the character of a lover, for which I had left so little room that he was quite baffled until he hit on the happy thought of throwing flowers to Eliza in the very brief interval between the end of the play and the fall of the curtain'.[12] It is significant that, whatever other ingenuities Tree may have perpetrated, the one Shaw cites is the attempt to modify, through the effect of stage business, what has always been *Pygmalion*'s most problematic aspect, its ending.[13]

That the play should conclude with the happy union of Higgins and Eliza would seem to be implied by its subtitle, *A Romance in Five Acts*, but at the beginning of the Postcript Shaw ignores the love-story element and announces that it is 'called a romance because the transfiguration it records seems exceedingly improbable'. However, Shaw could hardly have assumed that readers of the play, who come to the subtitle well before they come to the Postscript, would take the term 'romance' in this sense till he told them to do so. And in fact Shaw continues to send contradictory signals in the Postscript itself. He first says that Higgins remains 'one of the strongest personal interests' in Eliza's life, particularly as she is sure that no other woman is 'likely to supplant her with him'; later Shaw observes that Eliza is characteristically ill-tempered with Higgins and 'snaps his head off on the faintest provocation, or on none', telling us a moment after that 'She knows that Higgins does not need her, just as her father did not need her' but that 'his indifference is deeper than the infatuation of commoner souls'. Finally, Shaw claims that though in her fantasy life Eliza would like to drag Higgins 'off his pedestal and see him making love like any common man', she does not like him (or Mr Doolittle): 'Galatea never does quite like Pygmalion: his relation to her is too godlike to be altogether agreeable'.

But what has become an impossible tangle of ambiguous hints and contradictions in the discourse of the Postscript is held in perfect artistic stasis at the end of the play as Shaw wrote it. When Eliza, after asserting her independence, announces that she will not see Higgins again, he carelessly tells her to order a ham and Stilton cheese for the household and to buy him ties and gloves. Eliza's reply is intriguing, for she does not reject these tasks: she has already tended to some of them and evades, without refusing, the others. Her final line, 'What you are to do without me I cannot imagine', verges on being a confession that she is obliged to stay, just as Higgins' laughter at the prospect of her marrying Freddy may be either amusement at what he considers a ludicrous misalliance or a hilarious and disdainful rejection of the notion that it will actually occur. It is essential that these dubieties remain unresolved, for they are the dramatic analogues to the unresolvable Shavian conflicts that resonate through the play. That these conflicts have to do with familial and sexual matters is obvious enough from the passages quoted above, but they extend beyond these to social concerns as well. Like all of Shaw's great plays, *Pygmalion* deals with both social and personal affairs (granted that the emphasis here is on the latter), and as always the boundary between these areas is less clearly marked than one might expect.

Pygmalion does not at first glance seem like a socialist, much less a Fabian play, but it is. Higgins, who appears to notice little beyond his professional concerns, has noticed – no doubt in deference to the social interests of his author – with regard to flower girls and their like that 'a woman of that class looks like a worn out drudge of fifty a year after she's married'. Later Higgins explains to his mother that changing Eliza into a different being by 'creating a new speech for her' is 'filling up the deepest gulf that separates class from class and soul from soul'. These remarks, and especially the latter, cast a suggestive light on Act I, which is more than a charmingly imaginative prologue to the story of the 'squashed cabbage leaf' passed off as 'the Queen of Sheba'; it is a survey of the social, as well as linguistic distance Eliza must traverse from 'the gutter' with its 'kerbstone English' to the lower classes with their shrewd recognitions of marks of distinctions ('e's a genleman: look at his ba-oots') and latent hostility to the gentry ('You take us for dirt under your feet, dont you?'), to the shabby genteel (Shaw's own class) represented by the Eynsford-Hills, to the comfortable assurance of money and position embodied in Pickering. It is reasonable to suppose that the elimination of such nefarious social distinctions and the gradual – that is, Fabian – evolution of a classless society in which speech patterns are not a barrier is the ultimate aim of Higgins's Universal Alphabet, at least in Shaw's view (after all, the creation of a similar alphabet was the cause to which Shaw left his substantial estate). But the matter, being Shavian, does not end there. Egalitarianism is desirable not only to achieve social justice but for an even higher purpose: so that all shall be intermarriageable, that is, so that the Life Force can select couples from the total gene-pool of the population and thus have the widest latitude in breeding the Superman.

This consideration returns us again to the play's romantic, or in the full Shavian sense, sexual concerns. Eliza's demands, after she has by Higgins' efforts and her will been raised to a higher level of being, may have a metaphorical aspect, but that does not make them any less urgent. And from the point of view of the Life Force, Higgins would seem to be more suitable breeding material than Freddy. However, Higgins is not only a prospective father for Eliza's children, as her 'creator', he stands to some extent in a paternal relation to her already. Since Doolittle is her biological progenitor, Eliza has two fathers in the play, neither of whom, Shaw claims at the end of the Postscript, she likes. In actuality, Eliza addresses her father cosily as 'dad' in the last act and seems quaintly snobbish and jealous of his marrying her stepmother, 'that low common woman'. Nevertheless, she is glad enough to see the last of him in Act II, for she understands that he has come only to get money out of her new protectors and does not seem to understand, or sympathise with, his originality of character.

Since he has come to sell her for five pounds we pardon Eliza's insensitivity on this point even as we delight in the ingenuity with which Doolittle, one of Shaw's supreme comic creations, manipulates bourgeois sentimentality ('a father's heart, as it were') while seeing through the hypocrisies of 'middle-class morality', as in this proto-Brechtian exchange with Pickering, who is shocked at Doolittle's view of his daughter as a commercial property:

PICKERING: Have you no morals, man?
DOOLITTLE: [*unabashed*] Cant afford them, Governor. Neither could you if you was as poor as me.

(Doolittle should not be granted too much charm, however; compare the amiability of Stanley Holloway's performance as perpetuated in the film of *My Fair Lady* with the extra acerbity of Wilfred Lawson's characterisation, hinting at genuine coarseness and brutality, in the Pascal film of the play.) But despite his lack of 'morals' and his characterisation of himself as 'one of the undeserving poor', Doolittle seems cheerfully committed to the work ethic, assuring Higgins that he will spend the five pounds on a spree and will not 'live idle' on it (idleness, we recall, is Shaw's bête noire): 'I'll have to go to work same as if I'd never had it. It wont pauperize me, you bet'.

Perhaps it is this latent respectability, as well as his fear of the workhouse (his assurance that he already has to dye his hair to keep his job evokes Peter Shirley in *Major Barbara*), that makes him vulnerable to the bequest that Higgins partially thrusts upon him. For just as Higgins raises Eliza from the gutter to win a bet, so he elevates her father to make a joke. Not only are the actions parallel but they are neither of them motivated by a personal concern for the recipient. In both cases the results of this 'godlike' intervention are difficult to assess. Doolittle is saved from the workhouse, but he has lost his capacity for self-gratification, his 'happiness' as he repeatedly says (evidently without having learnt, like Marchbanks, to live without it). Moreover he must now marry his 'missus', who – in a delicious comic reversal of conventional romantic suppositions – has, he tells us, 'been very low, thinking of the happy days that are no more'. For the climax of Doolittle's story, as he goes off resplendently dressed to be married at St George's Hanover Square, is what many audiences have hoped would be the climax of his daughter's. Quite in the manner of an Elizabethan dramatist, Shaw makes the subplot of *Pygmalion* a darkly comic parody of the romantic element latent in the main plot.

In so doing, he achieves at least two artistic aims: he fulfils romantic expectations even as he teases them through the comic transmutation of the 'happy' ending, and by having Eliza's fleshly father marry, Shaw – through some magical process of compensation – relieves her spiritual father of the necessity of doing the same. (In this regard, compare the roles Shaw assigns to Jack Tanner and Don Juan.) That this relief should be granted is absolutely crucial to Shaw's instinctive strategy as he reworks the material of the Cinderella myth. Having been a rejected child who grew up to be one of the great public performers of the age, Shaw was deeply attracted to the story of the poor drudge who demonstrated her worthiness by dancing beautifully at the ball. But as the material of the play presented itself to his imagination, a considerable difficulty arose if the Fairy Godfather was to be identical with the Handsome Prince. The fantasy of parental beneficence associated with the former figure was hardly to be casually equated with the dream of erotic fulfilment embodied in the latter. Paradoxically, it is Shaw's sensitivity to these emotional resonances that leads him to modify the 'romantic' ending and thus open himself to the accusation of 'coldness'. A lesser writer would have had no hesitation in blurring these two figures and thus purveying a peculiar, though profoundly desired gratification to his audience.

The attraction between Higgins and Eliza is, nonetheless, very real, the more so, in fact, for being a dangerous one, and Shaw must try to find some dramatically viable reason for thwarting it. He offers a hint in the play, which he later expands. When Mrs Higgins complains that her son never falls in love with anyone under forty-five, he replies, 'My idea of a lovable woman is somebody as like you as possible'. Shaw explicates this suggestion in the Postscript, arguing that for an imaginative boy a mother with wealth, intelligence, grace, dignity, and artistic taste can effect 'a disengagement of his affections, his sense of beauty, and his idealism from his specifically sexual impulses'. In a post-Freudian age this notion seems somewhat naïve (though perhaps not Shaw's contention a moment later that for many people less fortunate in their upbringing 'literature, painting, sculpture, music, and affectionate personal relations come as modes of sex if they come at all') and apparently came to appear so to Shaw, who in 1939 described Higgins as 'a confirmed old bachelor with a mother-fixation', the latter term suggesting the recognition of a sexual element here.[14] At least as much to the point are Shaw's hints to the readers and performers in the stage directions near the beginning of the play describing Higgins as '*rather like a very impetuous baby*' and noting that '*he coaxes women as a child coaxes its nurse*', hints that are born out by Higgins' boyish impetuosity, his self-absorption, and his lack of adult social control. Higgins himself confesses to Pickering, 'Ive never been able to feel really grown-up and tremendous, like other chaps', and his mother addresses him and his colleague as, 'a pretty pair of babies, playing with your live doll'. In so far as Higgins' involvement with his mother is psychologically valid (and whatever Shaw's claims in the Postscript the text gives no more than a suggestion), it confirms what is dramatically pervasive in the play: that Higgins is, despite his forcefulness and his 'Miltonic' mind, a child playing at being a parent, a boy who has somehow become the father of a mechanical doll.

This view is less denigratory of Higgins than it may at first seem, for the artist/creator is, if not childish, often more in touch with his childhood than the average person (Dickens being only the most obvious example). As a characterisation of Eliza, the doll image is open to the objection that she is more 'human' than her mentor. This is, in effect, the point that Eliza herself raises in Act I ('Oh, youve no feeling heart in you: you dont care for nothing but yourself') and elaborates in Acts IV and V. Nevertheless, at Mrs Higgins' at home, the supreme mechanical perfection of Eliza's pronunciation and the programmed rigidity of her conversation about the weather ('The shallow depression in the west of these islands is likely to move slowly in an easterly direction') are, in contrast to the crudeness of her other discourse, the source of some of the richest comedy in the play. They also suggest another submerged myth that rises briefly to the surface here, that of the girl whose beauty infatuates her lover but who is then revealed as an exquisite puppet. (The most familiar artistic embodiments of this material are the ballet of *Coppelia* and Act I of Offenbach's *Les Contes d'Hoffman* – both derived from E. T. A. Hoffman's *Der Sandmann*.) For a moment Shaw, under the guise of comedy, touches on it as well, for he is sensitive to the masculine fears it embodies: that a woman is a different kind of creature – one without a soul – and to give her love leads to the dangerous possibility of losing one's own.

There is, however, another point of view from which Eliza seems to have too much rather than too little feeling, and that view has its myth as well. Eliza is both alluring and dangerous in her role as a woman, but it is not the only one she plays. Just as Shaw identifies with Higgins in his roles as teacher/parent/creator, so he identifies with Eliza in her role as child and sympathises with the demands she makes. Though Higgins claims, 'I have created this thing out of the squashed cabbage leaves of Covent Garden', he makes the mistake, usual in these circumstances, of failing to realise that his creation may rebel. 'But the monster', as Eric Bentley notes in discriminating the relevant myth here, 'turns against Frankenstein'.[15] Despite their obvious dissimilarities, the roots of Shaw's play extend into the same soil, or familial longing and frustration, that nourished Mary Shelley's tale. Her outcast creature, after all, acquired his power of speech – and the monster is extraordinarily eloquent – through observing an ideally affectionate family (the emotive failures, however whimsically presented, of her natural father are significant in accounting for Eliza's attachment to her surrogate one), and he turns finally against his creator when Frankenstein refuses to allow him love, to create for him a mate who will relieve his sense of solitude and rejection. That Higgins is a comic version of the mad scientist ('He's off his chump, he is', says Eliza in Act I 'I dont want not balmies teaching me') should not obscure the fact that he fails terribly, much as his nineteenth-century predecessor did, to recognise the responsibilities of a creator/parent (his attempt to calm his housekeeper's fears about Eliza is a – comic as always – case in point:

'You can adopt her, Mrs Pearce: I'm sure a daughter would be a great amusement to you').

But Eliza's childlike request for 'a little kindness' and her assurance that she is not making sexual demands ('Thats not the sort of feeling I want from you') are compromised by her insistence to Higgins a moment earlier that 'every girl has a right to be loved' and her boast that girls like her 'can drag gentlemen down to make love to them easy enough'. At the same time Higgins' exalted assurance that he has higher aims than personal affection ('I care for life, for humanity') and his denigration of the fleshly world, or as he calls it 'the life of the gutter' ('Work til youre more a brute than a human being; and then cuddle and squabble and drink til you fall asleep') are made doubtful by his obvious jealousy when Eliza discloses Freddy's infatuation with her: 'You have no right to encourage him'. Shaw deeply sympathises with Eliza as a rejected child even as he is both disquieted and allured by her as a woman. Higgins may be excused from being Eliza's lover on the grounds that he too is a child, but he is also a parent-figure ('Ah-ah-ah-ow-o-o! One would think you was my father'), a 'higher' father who rescues his downtrodden child but a dangerously possessive one. Wimpole Street, specified several times during the play as the location of Higgins' establishment, is, for persons with literary interests, best known as the address of another household with a gifted daughter named Elizabeth, who was held in thrall by a perversely jealous father. But Freddy is not adequate in the role of Robert Browning, and in any case Shaw's identification is with both father and daughter in all their tangled relationships. The ending of *Pygmalion* is remarkable not because it is elusive – it could hardly be otherwise – but because it holds in complex balance so much of the richness of the play.

Heartbreak House

In his next major play Shaw allows the father–daughter incest fantasy to achieve something like a happy culmination in the relationship between Captain Shotover and Ellie (Elizabeth?) Dunn, but now it is a subsidiary element in the play without much emotional weight and devoid of threatening sexuality. The personal themes of *Heartbreak House*, however, are mingled with other elements: a hint of Shaw's religious concerns and reflections of the political and military circumstances surrounding its composition. Despite Shaw's claim that he had begun *Heartbreak House* before the war (which would put it in the company of *Overruled* [1912], a thin comedy of flirtation, *The Music Cure* [1913], and *Great Catherine* [1913], farces on the theme of feminine strength and masculine weakness or foolishness), the Bodley Head edition dates its composition from March 1916 to May 1917, making it concurrent with the political farces that Shaw published as *Playlets of the War*. In any case, *Heartbreak House*, is, like the plays surrounding it, a comedy of sex and a comedy of politics, the latter aspect being ultimately less significant for the play as a whole but more immediately noticeable.

When Shaw's politico-economic views had entered his plays (and they did so less often than one might have expected of a committed socialist), they tended to be precise, as in the denigration of private charity in *Major Barbara*, and to a considerable degree optimistic: Perivale St Andrews is thus a vision of a society at once beneficent and economically efficient. But in *Heartbreak House* they are vague and apocalyptic. As a result, the play has a reputation for profundity that is somewhat misleading. In the nature of things, suggestions of impending disaster are likely to be correct politically, but that does not in itself make them admirable artistically. Captain Shotover's assurance that what Hector calls 'this ship that we are all in. . . . This soul's prison we call England', 'will strike and sink and split' is a sufficiently grave warning. But the metaphor here is the familiar one of the Ship of State, and Shotover's assertion that this ship can somehow be saved by giving it political direction in place of its present 'drifting' – 'Navigation. Learn it and live; or leave it and be damned' – is not only imprecise but lacks the poetic freshness of, for example, Undershaft's recipe for salvation, 'Money and Gunpowder'.

More intriguing is the sense of futility embodied in Mazzini Dunn who like his creator has 'joined societies and made speeches' which gives the play what is for Shaw an uncharacteristic sense of fatality and acceptance. 'Every year', Mazzini says, 'I expected a revolution or some frightful smash-up: it seemed impossible that we could blunder and muddle on any longer. But nothing happened, except of course, the usual poverty and crime and drink that we are used to'. 'Nothing ever does happen', he adds and assures Shotover, after the old captain's prediction of impending catastrophe, that 'nothing will happen'. Even the bombers that appear at the end of the play, and that Shotover greets with a shout of 'Something happening', do relatively little, nor are we sure whether the more thoughtful characters see them as a vitalising, if destructive force or merely as, in Hesione's words, 'a glorious experience' combining the thrill of danger and the relief of obliteration.

All of these elements, however, come crowding in near the end of the play, and thus, though they affect our final sense of its tone, they are not part of its continuing texture. The economic theme does run through the work as a whole, for it is clear from early on that Heartbreak House sustains itself precariously on the fringes of a capitalist society that values destruction above creation. Captain Shotover, who earns far more from his military inventions than from his beneficent ones, asks for 'deeper darkness' as he sets to work: 'Money', he says, 'is not made in the light'. But the play's representative capitalist, Boss Mangan, is far from the confident figure of power encountered in Andrew Undershaft, even in Sartorius and Sir George Crofts. A mere manager, afraid of his men and 'dreadfully afraid of being poor' (a very different matter from Undershaft's revulsion from poverty as a 'crime'), he lives on 'travelling expenses' along with 'a trifle of commission'; his schemes and the factories he supervises benefit others: 'syndicates and shareholders and all sorts of lazy good-for-nothing capitalists'. The Shavian denunciation of idleness remains unchanged, but for the moment capitalism appears as an obscure and complicated system unlikely to be altered by Mazzini Dunn and the inhabitants of Heartbreak House.

Nor do the Shavian religious ideas, which enter the play briefly, offer much prospect of betterment. Towards the end of Act I Hesione, Hector, and Captain Shotover bemoan their own failings and those of their world. When Hector asks despairingly, 'Is there no beauty, no bravery, on earth?' Hesione responds with a query of her own: 'What do men want?' (Characteristically Shaw reverses the genders of Freud's celebrated question, being, consciously at least, less concerned here with the frustrations of women than with those of men.) Since men have women's love and domestic comfort, she asks, why are they not satisfied: 'Why do they envy us the pain with which we bring them into the world, and make strange dangers and torments for themselves to be even with us?' The knowledgeable Shavian will recognise that the point here is not simply womb envy (to continue the Freudian analogy) but men's desire to partake in the procreative activity of the Life Force. Exactly that seems to have been Captain Shotover's aim in constucting Heartbreak House. In the play's next speech he chants two lines of verse:

> I built a house for my daughters, and opened the doors thereof,
> That men might come for their choosing, and their betters spring from their love.

But Shotover's evident hope that his daughters would become the agents of Creative Evolution appears to have been frustrated; one married a 'numskull', the other a 'liar', and the children we hear of seem to have no hint of the Superman about them.

Although Shaw's next extended work, *Back to Methuselah*, was to reaffirm and elaborate his faith, here he offers a sad and dubious reminiscence of *Man and Superman*. Indeed, from one point of view *Heartbreak House*, for all its darker coloration, is a direct descendant of that play. Despite Shaw's assertion in his sub-title that *Heartbreak House* is a *Fantasia in the Russian Manner*, there is very little about it that is Chekhovian. It is rather a disquisitory play like *Misalliance* (Billy Dunn, the burglar who is captured and becomes an embarrassment to the household, is a reworking of the would-be assassin of the earlier play), deriving ultimately from Act III of *Man and Superman*. In addition, an even more significant element links these plays together. The world of Heartbreak House is not centred on politics or religion; it is a sheltered world the inhabitants of which have time to occupy themselves with romantic dreams and unconsummated flirtations. Less fantastic but hardly less symbolic, it bears a notable resemblance to that Hell of love and beauty in which Don Juan and his friends discoursed on the higher meaning of sexuality.

The Don Juan who frequents the hell presided over by Shotover's 'two demon daughters' however, is no philosopher-amorist who explicates the workings of the Life Force and, as he prepares to ascend to a higher plane, dilates upon the lures of romance with lofty understanding. Since 'women are always falling in love with' his moustache, Hector Hushabye, who cannot fall in love himself, is regularly 'landed in all sorts of tedious and terrifying flirtations'. Unlike Higgins, another of Shaw's lovers of paternal age (Hector is a '*very handsome man of fifty*'), he has no work to save him; when not pursuing his flirtations, he is married 'up to the hilt' and 'at home all day, like a damned soul in hell'. If his given name suggests that he is at least a kind of hero condemned to this special underworld, his surname, hinting at childishness and sleep, suggests the futility of his heroic qualities. For all his genuine courage and gallantry, Hector remains a romantic lover, a Sergius Saranoff, still comically ineffective but older, sadder, more self-aware.

The woman with whom he conducts a flirtation in the course of the play also has emotional limitations. Ariadne Utterword begs her father to assure her that she has a heart to be broken, but her self-doubts are momentary, and before long she is announcing, in effect, that aristocratic authoritarianism will save England. Her political views and social attitudes, however, get little consideration except as subjects for easy jibes. Nor does her relationship with Hector come to more than a game of sexual teasing that both accept as such. It is her treatment of her perpetual pursuer, her brother-in-law Randall, that most importantly defines her status in the play. When Randall's jealousy makes him obstreperous, she calls him names till he bursts into helpless tears, whereupon she calls him 'cry-baby', explaining a moment later that this was the treatment she applied to her children when they 'got nerves and were naughty': 'a good cry and a healthy nervous shock'. Without receiving any sexual gratification (or perhaps receiving too much of a special kind), Randall is, in Hector's words, 'dragged about and beaten by Ariadne as a toy donkey is dragged about and beaten by a child'. Maternal dominance and childlike submission have appeared before in Shaw (one thinks at once of Candida and Morell) but hardly in so harsh a form.

But Ariadne is no monster of sexual perversity; like Candida she retains a genuine feminine charm. (She even has a certain comic flair, insisting with Wildean elegance that Heartbreak House needs horses and stables because 'there are only two classes in good society in England: the equestrian classes and the neurotic classes'.) Even more charming is her sister Hesione, the most alluring of all Shaw's embodiments of maternal eroticism. She too is witty: Shaw allows her to toss one of his most whimsical Shakespearean darts when teasing Ellie for her infatuation with one who, like Othello, tells tales of his exploits: 'Desdemona would have found him out if she had lived, you know. I wonder was that why he strangled her!' Hesione, however, has a darker nature as well and later confesses, 'when I am neither coaxing and kissing nor laughing, I am just wondering how much longer I can stand living in this cruel, damnable world'. Above all, Hesione resembles her sister ('Vampire women, demon women', Hector calls them only half-comically and later in the play, 'Daughters of the witch of Zanzibar') in her ability to reduce men to childishness and tears. When the unfortunate Mangan finds that Hesione had only given him 'the glad eye that time in the garden' to lure him away from Ellie, he '*sits down . . . on his chair and begins to cry like a child*' and bursts into tears again when she teasingly invites him for a romantic walk on the heath.

Nor does Mangan do much better with the ostensible heroine of the play, the heartbroken Ellie. Neither a 'siren' nor a 'gorgeous woman' like her older friend, Ellie does have the charm of youth, but that does not prevent her from being at least as ruthless with Mangan as Hesione. Although at first she seems about to sacrifice herself to 'a perfect hog of a millionaire for the sake of her father', by Act II she says she intends to 'make a domestic convenience' of Mangan, and in Act III she maintains that she had never really intended to make him marry her: 'I only wanted to feel my strength: to know that you could not escape if I chose to take you'. Once again, feminine power has demonstrated itself and reduced the male figure to impotence, for despite her infatuation with Hector, Ellie seems to suggest, in a disquieting moment, that sexuality is not a 'natural' part of adult relationships. She explains to Mangan in Act II that since she knows he is attracted to Hesione, she no longer objects to touching him: 'Not since you fell in love naturally with a grown-up nice woman, who will never expect you to make love to her'.

This abrogation of sexuality is carried to its ultimate conclusion and, to some degree, elucidated in Act III when Ellie announces her 'marriage' to Captain Shotover, her 'spiritual husband and second father'. The relationship, from one point of view hardly more than a playful sign of affection, is guarded from erotic reality by Shotover's lassitude and great age, but it nonetheless marks the culmination of a line of impassioned father-daughter relationships (real or symbolic) extending from Blanche,

Sartorius and her father through Cleopatra and Caesar, Barbara and Undershaft, Eliza and Higgins. Here, however, the dream of innocent incest is less significant than Ellie's alliance to Shotover's dissociation from life. The old captain preaches 'navigation', that is, will and social action, but in fact he 'cannot bear men and women'; he runs away, ostensibly to drink himself into awareness, but his effort is failing. 'I can feel nothing', he says, 'but the accursed happiness I have dreaded all my life long . . . the happiness of yielding and dreaming instead of resisting and doing'. Long before, one of Shaw's heroes had 'learned to live without happiness', but Marchbanks' withdrawal from domestic felicity had carried only a hint of morbidity. Nevertheless, all the Shavian saints had been, to some degree, dissociated from the world; Shotover approaching his deat3h and Ellie longing for the bombers are no more and no less beyond the world than the youngest and most active of those saints, Joan of Arc.

But before Shaw turned to that alluring but most problematic figure, he committed himself to a remarkable act of intellectual affirmation, the writing of the Metabiological Pentateuch', *Back to Methuselah,* which he began in March of 1918, while the war was still on, and worked on for two years. Unfortunately, however admirable it was to reassert under such circumstances his faith in the power of the Life Force to transcend mortal limitations, Shaw did not here produce the richly self-sustaining art work that he had in his previous 'metabiological' disquisition, *Man and Superman*. Although the Preface to *Back to Methuselah* remains Shaw's fullest, most brilliant exposition of his religious views, the arid stretches of the vast five-play cycle, which quite overwhelm its few lively moments, will not repay commentary.[16] The Elderly Gentleman, to whom death is mercifully granted because he 'cannot live among people to whom nothing is real' touches us for a moment by evoking the Shotover who 'cannot bear men and women', and the final part is an intriguing adumbration of some of the dystopias of science fiction. Indeed, the Ancients of that sad fantasy who have tired of tending to children – that is, to human beings with dreams of love and beauty – and who aspire to become vortices of 'pure intelligence', find that the earth is no place for such supra-mortal creatures as themselves – much as Shaw's Joan finds that it is no place for God's saints.

Saint Joan

Comparable discoveries had, of course, been made earlier by other Shavian 'saints', several of them young women, with similar results: Saint Vivie Warren had retired to her world of actuarial calculations, Saint Barbara Undershaft to her father's 'heavenly' city, and most recently Saint Ellie Dunn had joined her 'spiritual husband and second father' in his quest for the 'seventh degree of concentration', which by the end of the play is hardly to be distinguished from a desire for release from the mortal world. But the earlier dramatisations of this characteristic Shavian myth had not involved anything like the sentimental glamour of Joan's martyrdom. Although Shaw was careful to begin and end the play with scenes of farcical comedy and weight it in between with discourse on matters of church and state, he imbued it with enough emotive force so that it acquired a quite traditional kind of theatrical appeal. Audiences knew, or thought they knew, what to make of the Joan who inspires the Dauphin by announcing that she will 'dare, dare, and dare again, in God's name', and the play did well with them (less well with the critics) when it was produced in New York by the Theater Guild, with Winifred Lenihan creating the role of Joan, in December 1923, only a few months after it was written. It did well again the next year in London with Sybil Thorndike as Joan, and has remained a notable actress' vehicle (e.g. the revival with Katharine Cornell in 1936). Joan's canonisation came in 1920, the literary equivalent for Shaw in 1926 with the award of the Nobel Prize, granted in part no doubt because of the play's supposed 'heroic' quality.

Certainly Shaw's Joan, despite the play's comedy, can be taken straight as the tragic Maid of Orleans in a way that his whimsical Caesar cannot be as the conventional hero or lover. But when one looks closely at the rhetoric that supports this view of Joan, doubts begin to arise. In place of the heroic or poetic diction that one might expect, we find something quite different – much more characteristically Shavian. Joan's appeal to the Dauphin in Scene II (other passages could as easily be adduced) will do as an example:

> JOAN: [*earnestly*] Charlie: I come from the land, and have gotten my strength working on the land; and I tell thee that the land is thine to rule righteously and keep God's peace in, and not to pledge at the pawnshop as a drunken woman pledges her children's clothes. And I come from God to tell thee to kneel in the cathedral and solemnly give thy kingdom to Him for ever and ever, and become the greatest king in the world as His steward and His bailiff, His soldier and His servant. The very clay of France will become holy: her soldiers will be the soldiers of God: the rebel dukes will be rebels against God: the English will fall on their knees and beg thee let them return to their lawful

> homes in peace. Wilt be a poor little Judas, and betray
> me and Him that sent me?

In the hands of a gifted actress this speech works in the
theatre, not because it is fired by passion but because Shaw
has given Joan his own skills, those of the practised public
speaker. The colloquial opening ('Charlie') is followed by
a vivid simile, though the pawnshop and the drunken
woman probably owe more to nineteenth-century Dublin
than to medieval Lorraine. (The idealisation of the
peasantry – 'I come from the land' – is not what might be
expected of Shaw, but it makes for a familiar and effective
theatrical stance, though it has also made for some curious
attempts at theatrical realisation: Joan played in an Irish
brogue, Joan played by a black actress.) Then come the
balanced parallel phrases, 'His steward and His bailiff',
the striking antitheses, 'soldiers of God . . . rebels against
God', and a grand rhetorical question to top it off. But if
one compares these effects with, say, the overwhelming
colloquial vigour of the Devil's speech in *Man and
Superman*, they seem artful, even contrived.

In addition, Joan is recognisably a Shavian heroine in
more than her problematic rhetoric. She is a young woman
determined on a vocation that disturbs the values and
judgements of her elders. But the earlier Shavian heroines
whose circumstances are echoed in Joan's, Vivie Warren
and Barbara Undershaft, had proceeded to their destinies
through a richly various series of confrontations in which
they had found out much about the world and about
themselves. This is not the case in *Saint Joan*. Despite the
comic and intellectual vigour of many of its scenes, they
have a repetitive quality that prevents the play from
achieving the swift linearity of *Mrs Warren's Profession* or
Major Barbara. Indeed, one can argue that, aside from the

central disquisition on Joan as protestant and nationalist (Scene IV), there are in this most schematic of Shaw's plays only two scenes, each repeated three times. Not only do the three scenes that follow the confrontation between Warwick and Cauchon (Rheims Cathedral, the trial, and the Epilogue) offer a variation on the same theme but the three that precede it, despite their variety of event and character, do much the same.

They are the scenes of Joan's success. In each she asserts her will, demonstrates her power, and is accepted, admired, even revered by an authority figure. Indeed, the initial confrontation, that with de Baudricourt, is a characteristic scene of Shavian comedy in which a strong-minded woman sweetly and amiably reduces a self-important man to helpless impotence. Shaw caps it with a daring farcical apotheosis as the Steward rushes in announcing that the 'hens are laying like mad' and de Baudricourt crosses himself, superstitiously convinced that 'She did come from God'. At the end of the court scene, the extravagant snap of the fingers with which Charles dismisses La Trémouille and gives the command of the army to Joan ('Thourt answered, old Gruff-and-Grum') has something of the same effect, but now Joan has dealt with a different but still familiar Shavian figure, the physically weak and timid but cheeky and clever young man, a reworking not so much of Marchbanks as of Bentley Summerhays of *Misalliance*. At Orleans a different, though equally recognisable Shavian scene appears to be enacted: it is that in which a wise young soldier explains to an innocently enthusiastic girl the practicalities of war, and especially the foolishness of romantic heroism ('You must not dare a staff officer, Joan: only company officers are allowed to indulge in displays of personal courage'). The teacher-student fantasy that Shaw began in *Arms and the Man* is altered here (more happily than when the student asserted herself in *Pygmalion*); indeed it is reversed as the change in the wind proclaims Joan's status and Dunois kneels, handing her his baton: 'You command the king's army. I am your soldier'. In all of these scenes the central action is essentially the same: the ignorant country girl is revealed as a saint, the ugly duckling as a swan, the child of nature as truly the child of the ultimate Parent.

Within the play, however, the parental figures are far from beneficent. The scene between Warwick and Cauchon, the representatives of the greater families of church and state, does more than give the exhausted actress playing Joan a needed rest and dramatise an ingenious historical speculation, that Joan was the first protestant and nationalist. (And that point has less to do with Shaw's view of the past than with his evolutionary vision of the future, for the Joan who will teach her soldiers 'to fight that the will of God may be done in France' is an inspired agent of the Life Force impelling society to a higher form of organisation – compare Shaw's Don Juan declaring that a man will be careless of himself when he has 'a piece of what he calls God's work to do'.) Despite its being 'disquisitory', this scene, with the cautious jockeyings of Cauchon and Warwick counterpointed against the comic explosions of De Stogumber, has a higher degree of psychological tension than many another in the play. Moreover, the character of Warwick gives it a certain theatrical flair, for he is a familiar and appealing type (raised by Shaw to a higher power), the elegant, charmingly wicked nobleman, who wanders through so many of Oscar Wilde's plays (if Warwick would change his armour for evening dress, he could appear at Lady Windermere's *soirée* without causing even a raised eyebrow). But above all, this is the scene in which the figures of authority in the play determine that the rebellious child is to be punished for her presumption. Thus, this scene moves to a dramatic climax whereas the others are all, to greater or lesser degrees, epiphanies – exhibitions of Joan in saintly attitudes.

If the attitude displayed in the first three scenes has to do with triumph and acceptance, that which appears in the last three involves refusal and assertion, refusal of the earthly authorities to recognise Joan's true identity or to allow her a place among themselves and Joan's stubborn assertion of her superiority, of her status as the 'Dear-child-of-God'. In the Rheims Cathedral scene after she is rejected in order by the army, the monarchy, and the Church, Joan affirms her higher connections: 'it is better to be alone with God: His friendship will not fail me, nor His counsel, nor His love'. She says much the same thing near the end of the trial scene, though here she is even more explicit about the nature of these connections. Innocently astonished at finding that she is to be imprisoned, Joan takes back her recantation in one of Shaw's least successful 'poetic' speeches ('if only I could still hear the wind in the trees, the larks in the sunshine, the young lambs crying through the healthy frost. . . .'), but a moment later, when Ladvenu rebukes her with paternal anger as a 'wicked girl' and argues that if her instructions came from God He would free her, Joan's language abruptly intensifies, projecting not literary attitudes but genuine force: 'His ways are not your ways. He wills that I go through the fire to His bosom; for I am His child, and you are not fit that I should live among you. That is my last word to you'. Despite the biblical dignity of the opening phrases, this is the voice of the child desperately insisting on the reality of the 'family romance' (to appropriate Freud's term), the notion that it is not the child of its ostensible parents but of other and more exalted ones. It is the voice of the rejected child, rejecting in turn the parents who betray to be reunited with the Higher Parent who never will. When we recall that Shaw began his career as a dramatist by writing for *Widowers' Houses* a climactic scene in which a daughter passionately asserts the desire to remain with her beloved father and ends the greatest part of that career with a climactic assertion not so dissimilar as it might at first seem, we recognise again how central this material is to the Shavian vision of experience. Appropriately Shaw brings *Saint Joan* to a close as he replays the scene, barely disguised by its comedy, of Joan's rejection by the forces of authority and has Joan demand of the true parent when He will make the world into a home for his saintly child: 'O God that madest this beautiful earth, when will it be ready to receive Thy saints? How long, O Lord, how long?'

6
Last Plays:
'The Apple Cart' and After

After Shaw completed *Saint Joan* in 1923, he did not
return to the theatre with a new play for five years. This
extraordinary hiatus in his otherwise steady dramatic
productivity is in part accounted for by his work on the
grand summary of his economic views, *The Intelligent
Woman's Guide to Socialism and Capitalism*. Moreover,
during this period several significant events occurred in
swift succession. In 1925 Shaw received the Nobel Prize (he
usually declined honours, but he accepted this one, though
not the money, which was used to support the translation
of Swedish literature into English), and the next year he
passed his seventieth birthday. Hardly in a position to
know that he had almost a quarter of a century of good
health and intellectual vigour still before him, Shaw must
have felt, having already codified his ideas on religion in
Back to Methuselah, that *The Intelligent Woman's Guide*
was a culminating point in his career. And even more

significant than the Nobel Prize in testifying to the status he had achieved in his art was the founding of the Malvern Festival Theatre in 1929, largely to produce Shaw's plays.

But a theatre in which he could satisfy his dramatic inclinations free of the commercial requirements of the West End may not have been the most fortunate of gifts. To the structural looseness and reliance on verbal effects that Shaw had allowed himself in the Disquisitory Plays, he now added a taste for a kind of rambling fantasy with relatively little concern for performance values. How much of the casualness and curious remoteness of Shaw's later plays is due to a simple waning of his powers and how much to a self-indulgence induced by age and success is hardly possible to say. The result, in any case, was a body of work at once more and less 'serious' than the greater plays that had preceded it. Certainly there is an element of the carelessly playful in all of these works: many are fantasies of the future or of a past that never existed, some with grotesquely improbable plots or exotic locales. Even when Shaw brings the fascist dictators of the 1930s on stage, as in *Geneva*, they are mere political cartoons remote from the actual personalities whom they ostensibly represent, and they are presented in an entirely incredible circumstance – on trial before the International Court at The Hague. Yet it is just this persistent preoccupation with contemporary politics that leads these last works, despite their extravagance, to seem more earnest, though assuredly not more profound, than the earlier plays.

Ultimately, perhaps, the factor that more than any other makes the plays of Shaw's last period so anti-climactic is this radical change in subject matter. Despite the extraordinary variety of topics Shaw's plays had dealt with – slum landlordism, prostitution, eugenics, private charity, the practice of medicine, the importance of phonetics –

they had all been rooted in the central emotive relationships of sexual and familial life. However disguised by the range of his intellectual interests and coloured by the special quality of his temperament, these preoccupations had always in Shaw's works moved the action and focused the discussion. But in the last plays they seem tangential. Although none of them is without some reminiscence of the human concerns that had been the motive force of his previous work, most of the plays that Shaw wrote from 1928 till his death are directly or indirectly centred on the political questions that dominated the interregnum between the two World Wars.

To deal with such matters as the paralysing effects of party conflicts, governmental inefficiency, economic decay, and the rise of dictatorships as well as with wider philosophical questions associated with them, Shaw worked his own variations on a nineteenth-century theatrical mode, differing genres of which were called Burlesque, Opera Bouffe, and – the term appropriated by Shaw – Extravaganza.[1] The examples that survive in the twentieth-century performing repertoire are the operettas of Offenbach and of Gilbert and Sullivan. Foregoing the music (Gilbert had already foregone risqué humour and the presence of women in tights), Shaw took over the device of mixing satirically fanciful plots and settings with elements of contemporary reality as his way of commenting on the world in which he spent his final years. He called three of the eight full-length plays he produced after *Saint Joan* 'Extravaganzas', but in some measure the term suits them all.

Certainly it applies well to the first of them, *The Apple Cart*, which Shaw subtitled *A Political Extravaganza*. It is set in England and deals with conflicts between centres of governmental power, but it is a fantasy England of an indefinite future in which the King (Magnus), his Prime Minister (Proteus), and most of the other characters have exotically latinate names (Sempronius, Boanerges, etc.). The King has chosen the poetical 'Orinthia' for his mistress; his wife is a homey Queen Jemima. The major exception in nomenclature is Mr Vanhattan, the American ambassador, who in the concluding act distresses the King by announcing that the United States has decided to rejoin the British Empire. Despite Magnus' whimsically ironic suggestion that he and his countrymen might 'fight for our independence to the last drop of our blood', the ambassador assures him that the change is only nominal since England is already dominated by America's culture and economy. But Shaw has a wider subject than this shrewd, sadly humorous view of the altered relations between England and America. It is wider also than the prescient recognition that were the centre of political power to shift, it would move 'either west to Washington or east to Moscow' or the bitter view of British industry devoting itself to sweets, pottery, and sporting goods.

But his subject does have to do, in part at least, with Breakages, Limited, 'the biggest industrial corporation in the country', Shaw's symbol for the failure of capitalism (engaged in repair work, Breakages encourages inefficiency), which devotes itself to profits and power instead of constructive production. In addition, and even more to the point, it drains off the best talent from government, leaving behind the clownish or powerless creatures put in office by the ignorant mass electorate. Against these and their efforts to strip him of the residual power that he uses in the interests of the nation as a whole stands the playwright's image of the wise governor, King Magnus, who resembles Shaw's Caesar in his competence and his gentle charm. But whereas Caesar has the force of his legions behind him, Magnus is reduced to maintaining his position by an ingeniously improbable political manoeuvre (he threatens to abdicate, become a commoner, and lead an opposition party in Parliament). Like Magnus is beleaguered by those who cannot understand his wisdom and, momentarily, bedazzled by women. He spends an interlude, irrelevant to the plot, in what he calls 'fairyland', displaying his 'strangely innocent' relations with his beautiful mistress. She, however, complains that when 'the gates of heaven' open before him (perhaps those same gates through which Eugene Marchbanks had refrained from passing over thirty years before), he turns back to the world of domestic life and governmental responsibility.

But these reminiscences of the earlier Shavian vision are fleeting. Essentially *The Apple Cart* remains the paradigmatic late Shaw play: haphazard in plot, thin in characterisation, fantastic in tone, public in orientation. However individual in some ways, the works that follow, which may be considered more briefly, all show these characteristics. Shaw called *Too True to be Good* (1931), like *The Apple Cart*, a 'Political Extravaganza', but most of its fantasy is more personal. In Act I it takes the form of a human-sized talking microbe in the bedroom of a coddled young woman. When a burglar and his female accomplice try to steal her necklace, she escapes from her hypochondria (a Shavian fate of the idle rich) by joining them and running off with the necklace herself. Act II, set in a nameless tropical locale where the Patient – now restored to vigorous health – and her friends have travelled while spending their stolen gains, is enlivened by a charming caricature of Shaw's friend T. E. Lawrence ('of Arabia'), presented here as Private Meek, the unassuming master of military and administrative efficiency. But the most striking passage in the play is the final one, a momentary evocation of some of the grimmer passages in *Heartbreak House*. In a long speech to the audience the burglar, now become a preacher, 'the new Ecclesiastes', facing the post-war collapse of the older beliefs, cries, 'I must have affirmations to preach' but then continues despairingly:

> I am ignorant: I have lost my nerve and am intimidated: all I know is that I must find the way of life, for myself and all of us, or we shall surely perish. And meanwhile my gift has possession of me: I must preach and preach and preach no matter how late the hour and how short the day, no matter whether I have nothing to say –

Though in his peroration the preacher hopes for an inspiring message that will establish 'the Kingdom and the Power and the Glory', Shaw himself noted in a concluding comment that 'fine words butter no parsnips'. He protested later that the despair here expressed was the character's and not his, but the sorrow rings true and the protestation does not. He fought off the despair, yet it never entirely left his consciousness.

It returned in his next play, *On the Rocks* (1933), set in an England at once fantastic (a liberal Prime Minister is converted to socialism after retiring to a 'retreat' in Wales to meditate and study under the aegis of a mysteriously robed Lady Doctor) and more than real (swarms of the unemployed roam through London and are beaten by the police outside the Cabinet Room at 10 Downing Street, where the play is set). When the Prime Minister, an amiable talker called Sir Arthur Chavender, returns and presents the programme of socialist action that will save the country, he is soon deserted by the conservative factions in Parliament, on which he depends. His distress is echoed by Old Hipney, a 'revolutionary Socialist' now so disillusioned with the enfranchised workers who have 'booted out at the polls' those who have served them that he wishes 'for any Napoleon or Mussolini or Lenin or Chavender that has the stuff in him to take both the people and the spoilers and the oppressors by the scruffs of their silly necks and just sling them into the way they should go with as many kicks as may be needful to make a thorough job of it'. Hipney grants the people 'a choice between qualified men' but seems to see force or force of character as the means of distinguishing quality. ('The Jews didnt elect Moses: he just told them what to do and they did it'.) Chavender accepts the argument but recognises that he is 'not the man for the job': 'And I shall hate the man who will carry it through', he says to his wife, 'for his cruelty and the desolation he will bring on us and our like'.

Presumably because it has fewer elements of the bizarre, Shaw called *On the Rocks* not an 'Extravaganza' but a 'Political Comedy'. In his next two plays, which are more overtly personal, he dispensed with 'political' subtitles, but these works have such resonance none the less. *The Simpleton of the Unexpected Isles* (1934), set in the tropical reaches of the British Empire at some point in the future, concerns a eugenic experiment among two British couples and a priest and priestess of an unspecified eastern religion (evidently the worship of the Life Force), whose polygamous union is intended to produce a more exalted species (for Shaw this always implies one capable of rational government) but results only in four beautiful, vaguely oriental offspring, symbolic representatives of Love, Pride, Heroism, and Empire. However, the union of the two girls of this group with the Simpleton, an innocent young English clergyman (a sort of cross between Parsifal, the Holy Fool, and the earnest hero of *The Pirates of Penzance* – he has been carried about by a band of brigands) is sterile, and Shaw simply tacks on an ending to his play by having a very matter-of-fact Angel arrive to announce the Day of Judgement (or rather Year; it's a long business) has arrived and that those who are idle are the first to be obliterated. A similar eugenic effort seems to be at hand in *The Millionairess*, written in a creative burst immediately after *The Simpleton*. Once again the subject is the union of the worldly energy of the West, symbolised by the money-making and organisational talents of the Millionairess, Epifania Ognisanti di Parerga, with the spirituality and compassion of the Egyptian Doctor whom she determines to marry. The dramatic fantasy is provided by the parentally imposed tests in the handling of money (a reminiscence of the sort of folkloric motif reflected in *The Merchant of Venice* and even to some degree in *Major Barbara*), although Epifania's labours, which are dramatised, allow Shaw an excursion into sweatshop economics. Finally the epiphany granted to the reluctant Doctor is that the irresistible heartbeat of the heroine ('the life! the pulse!') is that of Allah himself, which is to say the very pulsation of the Life Force, and that he cannot give it up.

But *The Millionairess* has a political dimension as well as a religious one, for Epifania is a natural 'boss', a dictator in her own realm, who ruthlessly clears away the old life to construct a new economic order. She is a fantasy vision of what Arthur Chavender of *On the Rocks* was too gentle to be, the person 'for the job'. In *Geneva* (1936), subtitled *Another Political Extravaganza*, Shaw brought on stage the three such persons who dominated the politics of Europe in the 1930s: Mussolini (as 'Bombardone'), Hitler (as 'Battler'), and Franco (as 'Flanco de Fortinbras'). However, these figures are Shavian speechmakers, reflecting little of the historical personalities on which they are based and doing little beyond taking part in a rambling discussion (in a post-Holocaust era Battler's defence of anti-Semitism, however remote from Shaw's views, makes painful reading) that leads only to the familiar Shavian assertions that 'Man is a failure as a political animal' and must be succeeded by 'something better', followed by the threat, never realised however, of a new ice age.

A vastly more attractive political discourse is to be found in the last play Shaw completed before World War II, '*In Good King Charles's Golden Days*'. Liberated perhaps by the historical subject, Shaw suddenly found himself in the position of a great opera singer near the end of his career when, on an occasional night, his powers return once more and the voice catches its earlier sweetness. Not the most dramatic of Shaw's conversation pieces nor the most intellectually compelling, *King Charles* is quite the most charming and one unduly neglected by producers. When Charles, incognito as 'Mr Rowley', pays a visit to Isaac Newton at the scientist's house in Cambridge, he is joined by his brother, the future James II, George Fox (founder of the Society of Friends), the painter Godfrey Kneller, and assorted mistresses: the characterisations are lightly but surely sketched; the humour is amiable, and the conversation moves gracefully from science to religion, art, love, and politics. But in the brief Act II, a touching image of domestic affection between Charles and his Queen, Catherine of Braganza, the political skies darken again, and Charles tells her wearily, 'the riddle of how to choose a ruler is still unanswered; and it is the riddle of civilization', explaining his own popularity by the fact that he enjoys himself and leaves things 'as they are, though things as they are will not bear thinking of by those who know what they are'.

At the beginning of Shaw's last full-length play, *Buoyant Billions* (completed in 1947 but begun in 1936 and later put aside) a young man has resolved to be a 'world betterer' and attempt to alter, or at least denounce, 'things as they are', but the play drifts along from a romantic adventure to a Shavian discussion and finally to an affirmation of the impulses of the Life Force and the hope for a future in which intellectual ecstacy will surpass physical pleasure and even spirtual exaltation. *Buoyant Billions* is not the last of Shaw's plays. That is *Why She Would Not*, 'A Little Comedy' as Shaw called it, finished shortly before the fall in his garden that ultimately ended his life in 1950 and forming part of the body of juvenilia, occasional sketches, and other works appended to the Shavian canon.

More endearing is Shaw's last regularly published play, what he said would 'in all actuarial probability' be his final work, a ten-minute, blank-verse skit for puppets, written at the request of a Malvern puppeteer, called *Shakes versus Shav* (1949). It is a madly whimsical conflict in which each figure knocks the other down and offers excerpts from his work in comic self-justification. Finally Shav cries, 'Peace, jealous Bard:/We are both mortal. For a moment suffer/My glimmering light to shine'. Shakes ends the playlet by puffing out the light that has appeared between them as he exclaims 'Out, out, brief candle'.

It is significant that for all his half-playful assertiveness, Shaw, at this valedictory moment of his career, felt the weight of the 'jealous Bard' (he mischievously shifts his own feeling to his rival), the great presence that no English playwright can readily put by. Shaw may lack Shakespeare's tragic vision and poetic power, yet in their place he offers us a uniquely exuberant rhetorical style, a remarkable intellectual range, a sweetness and fecundity of comic invention, and a startling sense of the complexity of erotic and familial connections. His 'glimmering light' cannot so easily be extinguished.

Notes

1. The Life

1. Passages from Shaw's extensive autobiographical writings have been arranged in a coherent sequence by Stanley Weintraub and published as *Shaw: An Autobiography* (New York: Weybright and Talley, 1969). The first volume covers the years from 1856 to 1898; the second runs from 1899 to 1950. The sections here quoted are from vol. I, pp. 11, 22, and 36.

2. All quotations from Shaw's plays in this study are taken from Dan H. Laurence (ed. supervisor), *The Bodley Head Bernard Shaw*, 7 vols (London: Max Reinhardt, 1970–74).

3. 'Biographic: G. B. S. (70) on George Bernard Shaw (20)', in R. J. Kaufmann (ed.), *G. B. Shaw: A Collection of Critical Essays*, (Englewood Cliffs, New Jersey: Prentice-Hall, 1965) p. 21.

4. Daniel Dervin argues in psychoanalytic terms that the early deprivation of maternal nurture and affection was crucial in the development of the Shavian personality and ethos because of the transformation of the idea of the lost, idealised mother in the mind of a child so treated. 'Whatever its components', he says, 'the maternal image turns into the ego-ideal and subsequently the object of narcissistic libido'. Thus Dervin suggests that both the aspirations and the impulsive, self-gratifying energy of Shaw as a child would have focused themselves on the personal qualities of the mother. See *Bernard Shaw: A Psychological Study* (Lewisburg, Pennsylvania Bucknell University Press, 1975) p. 68.

5. B. C. Rosset not only postulates adultery but suggests that Shaw

213

may have been Lee's natural son. Although Rosset is a diligent researcher on many matters, this conjecture seems unlikely. See *Shaw of Dublin: The Formative Years* (University Park, Pennsylvania: Pennsylvania State University Press, 1964).

6. Maurice Valency, *The Cart and the Trumpet* (New York: Oxford University Press, 1973) p. 9.

7. Quoted by R. F. Rattray in *Bernard Shaw: A Chronicle* (London: Leagrave Press, 1951) p. 44.

8. Ibid., pp. 53–4. Letter of E. Nesbit (Mrs Hubert Bland).

9. 'The Author's Apology' to *Our Theatres in the Nineties*. For further comment on Shaw's drama criticism see Chapter 3.

10. Shaw's diary as quoted in St John Ervine, *Bernard Shaw: His Life, Work and Friends*, (London: Constable, 1956) p. 153.

11. Letter of 14–15 June 1897, in Dan H. Laurence (ed.) *Collected Letters, 1874–1897*, (London: Max Reinhardt, 1965) p. 775. Where possible, quotations from Shaw's letters in this study are drawn from this volume and its successor, *Collected Letters, 1898–1910* (1972).

2. The Life of the Intellect

1. See Julian Kaye, *Bernard Shaw and the Nineteenth-Century Tradition* (Norman: University of Oklahoma Press, 1958) pp. 9–25.

2. The case for the influence of Mill and the Utilitarians is well put by William Irvine in *The Universe of G. B. S.* (New York: McGraw-Hill, 1949) pp. 51–74.

3. 'Darwin and Karl Marx', Preface to *Back to Methuselah, The Bodley Head Bernard Shaw* vol. v, p. 315.

4. 'The Basis of Socialism: Economic', in *Fabian Essays in Socialism* (London: George Allen & Unwin, 1948) p. 17.

5. Ibid., p. 21.

6. For comments on the relationship of the Fellowship to the Fabian ideal of service to an exalted cause, see Robert Skidelsky, 'The Fabian Ethic', in Michael Holroyd (ed.) *The Genius of Shaw* (London: Hodder and Stoughton, 1979) pp. 113–28.

7. 'Fabian Tract No. 41: The Fabian Society: What It Has Done and How It Has Done It', in C. E. M. Joad (ed.) *Shaw and Society: An Anthology and a Symposium* (London: Odhams Press, 1953) p. 77.

8. Anne Fremantle, *This Little Band of Prophets: The British Fabians* (New York: New American Library, 1959) p. 46.

9. 'Fabian Tract No. 41', p. 85. Even in later years the society remained comparatively small; in 1909, for example, the London membership was little over one thousand.

10. Irvine, p. 86.

11. Ibid., p. 90.

Notes

12. 'Sixty Years of Fabianism: A Postscript', *Fabian Essays*, pp. 222, 229.

13. *The Intelligent Woman's Guide to Socialism, Capitalism, Sovietism and Fascism* (Harmondsworth: Penguin, 1937) pp. 491, 492.

14. *Bernard Shaw* (Norfolk, Connecticut: New Directions, 1947) p. 31.

15. *The Intelligent Woman's Guide*, pp. 91, 90.

16. 'The Simple Truth about Socialism', in Louis Crompton (ed.) *Bernard Shaw: The Road to Equality: Ten Unpublished Lectures and Essays, 1884–1918* (Boston, Massachusetts: Beacon Press, 1971) pp. 185, 186.

17. Preface to *Back to Methuselah*, p. 308.

18. This phrase, from the section 'The Betrayal of Western Civilization' in the Preface to *Back to Methuselah*, was later deleted by Shaw and therefore does not appear in the Bodley Head edition. See *Bernard Shaw: Complete Plays with Prefaces* vol. II, (New York: Dodd, Mead, 1962) LXX.

19. See Shaw's charming religious fable *The Black Girl in Search of God* for a whimsical view of the Old Testament incarnations of the divinity as well as of later religious and philosophical ideas. For a lively Shavian discussion of the Gospels and of the character of Jesus – who is presented as a bohemian, a socialist, and a believer in the Life Force – see the Preface to *Androcles and the Lion*.

20. Preface to *Back to Methuselah*, p. 294.

21. *Philosophie Zoologique*, quoted in Butler's *Evolution, Old and New* (London: Jonathan Cape, 1924) pp. 230–1.

22. *Evolution, Old and New*, pp. 27–8.

23. See Kaye, *Bernard Shaw and the Nineteenth-Century Tradition*, pp. 54–9.

24. Quoted in *Evolution, Old and New*, p. 238.

25. *Unconscious Memory* (London: Jonathan Cape, 1924) p. 238.

26. *Luck, or Cunning?* (London: Jonathan Cape, 1922) p. 78.

27. Ibid., p. 20.

28. *The Sanity of Art*, in *Major Critical Essays, The Works of Bernard Shaw* (London: Constable, 1930) p. 323.

29. Kaye, *Bernard Shaw and the Nineteenth-Century Tradition*, pp. 49–53. See pp. 49–131 for a broad consideration of Shaw's place in the religious thought of the age.

30. The story, deriving from Bertrand Russell's *Portraits from Memory*, is presented by J. Percy Smith in *The Unrepentant Pilgrim: A Study of the Development of Bernard Shaw* (Boston: Houghton Mifflin, 1965) p. 147.

31. *Thus Spake Zarathustra*, R. J. Hollingdale (Trans.), (Harmondsworth: Penguin, 1961) pp. 41–2.

3. The Life of the Theatre

1. For a thoughtful discussion of the relation between Shaw's temperament and his style, see Richard Ohmann, *Shaw: The Style and the Man* (Middletown, Connecticut: Wesleyan University Press, 1962).

2. Shaw's reviews may be found in *Our Theatres in the Nineties*, the volumes of his drama criticism originally published in *The Saturday Review*, included in the collected editions of his works.

3. From a letter to Ivor Brown, quoted in his *Shaw in His Time* (London: Nelson, 1965) p. 40.

4. Something like Shaw's prescription was finally realised in the controversial version of *The Ring* done at Bayreuth in 1976.

5. The phrase occurs in a letter to James Huneker, *Collected Letters 1898–1910,* p. 505.

6. Quotations from Wagner's librettos are taken from the *Sämtliche Schriften und Dichtungen* (Leipzig: Breitkopf & Härtel [etc], 1912–14). I have argued the Wagnerian parallels here discussed in much greater detail in 'The Playwright as Perfect Wagnerite: Motifs from the Music Dramas in the Theatre of Bernard Shaw,' *Comparative Drama*, XIII (1979) 187–209.

7. These matters are admirably clarified by J. L. Wisenthal in the introduction to his *Shaw and Ibsen* (Toronto: University of Toronto Press, 1979.) Wisenthal reprints, along with the text of *The Quintessence*, the direct warnings to rival socialists that Shaw omitted from the published version and footnotes the changes (which are perhaps less significant than Wisenthal argues) that, despite his disclaimers, Shaw did indeed make when he added new material to *The Quintessence* in 1913. This is the best edition in which to read *The Quintessence*.

8. See Charles A. Carpenter, *Bernard Shaw and the Art of Destroying Ideals* (Madison: University of Wisconsin Press, 1969).

9. These equivalences and many others are thoughtfully examined in Martin Meisel's *Shaw and the Nineteenth-Century Theater* (Princeton: Princeton University Press, 1963).

10. The text of Sardou's play, along with photographs of the kind of heavily realistic settings that, Shaw complained, took so long to assemble, may be found in *L'illustration théâtrale* for 1907, no. 75.

11. For a full consideration of both these topics see two studies by Bernard Dukore: *Bernard Shaw, Director* (Seattle: University of Washington Press, 1971) and *The Collected Screenplays of Bernard Shaw* (Athens: University of Georgia Press, 1980).

4. Plays of the Nineties

1. *The Bodley Head Bernard Shaw* vol. I, p. 46.

2. 'Beware of the scribes, which love to go in long clothing, and love

Notes

salutations in the market places, and the chief seats in the synagogues, and the uppermost rooms at feasts: Which devour widows' houses, and for a pretence make long prayers; these shall receive greater damnation'. Mark Chapter XII, verses 38–40. The 'long clothing' is evidently, with an ironic glance at *Sartor Resartus,* the source of Sartorius' curious name.

3. From Shaw's diary, quoted in *Collected Letters 1874–1897*, p. 296.

4. 'A Dramatic Realist to His Critics', an essay originally published in the July issue of *The New Review*. See *The Bodley Head Bernard Shaw* vol I, pp. 490–1.

5. Alan Dent (ed.), *Bernard Shaw and Mrs Patrick Campbell: Their Correspondence* (New York: Knopf, 1952) pp. 92–5.

6. Letter of Mansfield, quoted in Valency, p. 119.

7. See Meisel, pp. 226–33 and Valency, pp. 120, 128–9.

8. Letter to the *Evening Standard*, 30 November 1944, quoted in Margery M. Morgan, *The Shavian Playground* (London: Methuen, 1972) p. 65.

9. In this cryptic, rather Hegelian passage Shaw seems to be suggesting that Christian Socialism will be succeeded by higher forms of thought and action that unify religious aspiration and social conscience. Presumably such advances will be adumbrated by Marchbanks as philosopher–artist and will resemble Shaw's more radical socialism and his Life Force religion. See Keegan's speech at the end of *John Bull's Other Island* for what is undoubtedly Shaw's own mystic vision of the unity of church and state.

10. *Collected Letters, 1847–1897*, pp. 623, 632. There are also references to Candida as Virgin Mother in the play's original draft.

11. *The Shavian Playground*, p. 77. Berenson's *Italian Painters of the Renaissance* appeared in 1894. It has been pointed out to me that the swarm of *putti* below the Virgin evoke the hundreds of 'strong sweetheart sons' of the extraordinary sexual fantasy in Shaw's letter to Ellen Terry quoted earlier. *Collected Letters, 1874–1897*, pp. 774–5.

12. Letter to James Huncker, *Collected Letters, 1898–1910*, p. 415.

13. *Candida* (New York: Bobbs-Merrill, 1973) p. XVII.

14. See Chapter 3 above for further discussion of Shaw as Wagnerite.

15. From a letter by Shaw to a group of schoolboys at Rugby who had written to him asking about Marchbank's secret. George A. Riding, 'The Candida Secret' in *The Spectator*, 185 (November 1950), 506. Reprinted in the Bobbs-Merrill *Candida*.

16. From *Sartor Resartus*, 'The Everlasting Yea'. The idea of being able to do without happiness was obviously deeply significant to Shaw. He was to use it again in *The Perfect Wagnerite*; and in a letter on the role of Candida to Janet Achurch, in which he recommends religious devotions as an alternative to drink and morphia, he argues that really religious people are 'able to do without happiness'. *Collected Letters 1874–1897*, p. 504.

17. *Bernard Shaw and the Art of Destroying Ideals*, p. 148.

18. See Cyril Maude, *The Haymarket Theatre* (London: Grant Richards, 1903) pp. 211–17. The chapter, written in the persona of Maude, is included in Vol. I of *The Bodley Head Bernard Shaw* and as an Appendix in Vol. I of the Weintraub/Shaw *Autobiography*.

19. Quoted by Valency, pp. 157–8.

20. See Valency, p. 160.

21. See *The Bodley Head Bernard Shaw* Vol II, p. 146 and the *Collected Letters 1874–1897*, p. 734.

22. See Shaw's letters to Siegfried Trebitsch of 25 June and 7 May 1906. *Collected Letters 1898–1910*, pp. 629–31.

23. 'Bernard Shaw and the Heroic Actor', in *The Bodley Head Bernard Shaw* Vol. II, p. 307.

24. For background on this matter see Louis Crompton, *Shaw the Dramatist* (Lincoln: University of Nebraska Press, 1969) pp. 60–3, 231–5.

5. Plays of Maturity

1. The problem in staging the complete *Man and Superman* is not the patience of the audience but the endurance of the leading actor. Under repertory circumstances, when Tanner/Don Juan need not act every day, performances of the entire work are perfectly feasible. Those who were privileged to see the transcendent realisation of the complete role by Ian Richardson at the Shaw Festival, Niagara-on-the-Lake, Canada, in the summer of 1977 find it difficult to be content with truncated versions.

2. Such critics as Robert Brustein and J. L. Wisenthal have with different emphases pointed to contrasting elements in Shaw's temper and work. See respectively *The Theatre of Revolt* (Boston: Little, Brown, 1964) and *The Marriage of Contraries: Bernard Shaw's Middle Plays* (Cambridge, Massachusetts: Harvard University Press, 1974).

3. Letter by Shaw to Harley Granville-Barker, 24 August 1904. *Collected Letters 1898–1910*, p. 444. See also letters to and from W. B. Yeats, pp. 452–3.

4. Most of these parallels are noted by Wisenthal in *The Marriage of Contraries*, p. 96.

5. *Collected Letters 1898–1910*, p. 444.

6. Henderson, *George Bernard Shaw* (Cincinnati: Steward, 1911) p. 381, quoted in Charles A. Berst, *Bernard Shaw and the Art of Drama* (Urbana, University of Illinois Press, 1973) p. 159.

7. Shaw was aware that the last act was problematic even as *Major Barbara* was being written. See his letters to Gilbert Murray and J. E. Vedrenne for 1, 2, and 7 October 1905. *Collected Letters 1898–1910*, pp. 564–5.

8. The model for Lady Britomart was Lady Rosalind Howard, Countess of Carlisle, who was the mother-in-law of the model for Cusins,

Gilbert Murray. For informative comment on the relationship between the characters and their prototypes see Crompton, pp. 105–10.

9. The relations between *The Doctor's Dilemma* as both domestic and medical drama, and its predecessors is ably discussed by Meisel, pp. 233–41.

10. Shaw's identification with Dubedat is an uneasy one, as suggested by his ambiguous treatment of the painter's death. Dubedat's statement of allegiance to Michael Angelo, Velasquez, and Rembrandt seems to be an aestheticised, but quite serious adaptation of the speech of a dying musician in Wagner's story 'An End in Paris', whose commitment is to God, Mozart, and Beethoven. But in the midst of dignified pronouncements Shaw allows Dubedat to lapse into schoolboy clichés: 'But Ive played the game. Ive fought the good fight'. These may pass by in performance, but not the perfectly calculated laugh (and careful reminder of Dubedat's vanity) as Walpole bemusedly reports his last, faint words: 'He wants to know is the newspaper man here'.

11. *Our Theatres in the Nineties*, 11 January 1896. The Christans' 'strange, perverted voluptuousness' evaded Shaw but not the desire for 'escape from the world'.

12. 'H. Beerbohm Tree: From the Point of View of the Playwright', reprinted in *The Bodley Head Bernard Shaw* vol. IV, p. 811.

13. The most notorious attempt to 'repair' the ending of *Pygmalion* is to be found at the conclusion of the film version, whose makers with fearful ingenuity used Shaw's own dialogue to patch up a version in which Eliza ultimately returns to a lovelorn Higgins. For full details of this curious story see Dukore, *The Collected Screenplays of Bernard Shaw*, pp. 82–5.

14. 'Bernard Shaw Flays Filmdom's "Illiterates"', reprinted in *The Bodley Head Bernard Shaw* vol. IV. p. 822.

15. *Bernard Shaw*, p. 121.

16. Readers interested in a defence of *Back to Methuselah* as a drama will find it in Morgan, pp. 221–38.

6. Last Plays

1. See Meisel, pp. 380–428 for a detailed discussion of these genres and Shaw's use of their characteristic devices.

Bibliography

1. Works by Shaw

The Bodley Head Bernard Shaw Dan H. Laurence (ed. supervisor) 7 vols
(London: Max Reinhardt, 1970–74). This is the best edition in which to
read Shaw's plays. His music criticism has been published and his
drama criticism is to be made available in the same format. For wider
reading in Shaw the 'Standard' edition published by Constable is the
best and most nearly complete.

Collected Letters 1874–1897, 1898–1910 Dan H. Laurence (ed.) (London:
Max Reinhardt, 1965, 1972). Further volumes of Shaw's letters are to
be published. Separate editions of his correspondence with Frank
Harris, Granville-Barker and others are available; the two best known
of such collections are listed below.

Ellen Terry and Bernard Shaw: A Correspondence Christopher St John
(ed.) (New York: G. P. Putnam's Sons, 1932).

Bernard Shaw and Mrs Patrick Campbell: Their Correspondence Alan
Dent (ed.) (New York: Knopf, 1952).

Shaw: An Autobiography 1856–1898, 1898–1950. Selected from his
writings by Stanley Weintraub. (New York: Weybright and Talley,
1969, 1970).

*Bernard Shaw: The Road to Equality: Ten Unpublished Lectures and
Essays, 1884–1918*. Louis Crompton (ed.) (Boston, Massachusetts:
Beacon Press, 1971).

Collected Screenplays of Bernard Shaw Bernard Dukore (ed.) (Athens:
University of Georgia Press, 1980).

Bibliography

Fabian Essays in Socialism (London: George Allen and Unwin, 1948). Essays by Shaw and others.

The Intelligent Woman's Guide to Socialism, Capitalism, Sovietism and Fascism (Harmondsworth: Penguin, 1965).

The Quintessence of Ibsenism in J. L. Wisenthal, *Shaw and Ibsen* (Toronto: University of Toronto Press, 1979).

2. Biography

The two most comprehensive biographies of Shaw, those by Ervine and Henderson, are listed below, but neither is fully satisfactory. Michael Holroyd's biography, authorised by the Shaw estate, will in time almost certainly supersede them.

Ervine, St John, *Bernard Shaw: His Life, Work and Friends* (New York: William Morrow, 1956).

Henderson, Archibald, *George Bernard Shaw: Man of the Century* (New York: Appleton, 1956).

Pearson, Hesketh, *G. B. S.: A Full Length Portrait* (Garden City, New York: Garden City Publishing Co, 1942).

Rattray, R. F., *Bernard Shaw: A Chronicle* (London: Leagrave Press, 1951).

Rosset, B. C., *Shaw of Dublin: The Formative Years* (University Park: Pennsylvania State University Press, 1964).

Weintraub, Stanley, *Journey to Heartbreak: The Crucible Years of Bernard Shaw 1914–1918* (New York: Weybright and Talley, 1971).

3. Criticism: Books

Bentley, Eric, *Bernard Shaw* (Norfolk, Connecticut: New Directions, 1947).

Berst, Charles A., *Bernard Shaw and the Art of Drama* (Urbana: University of Illinois Press, 1973).

Boxill, Roger, *Shaw and the Doctors* (New York: Basic Books, 1969).

Carpenter, Charles A., *Bernard Shaw and the Art of Destroying Ideals: The Early Plays* (Madison: University of Wisconsin Press, 1969).

Chesterton, G. K., *George Bernard Shaw* (New York: Hill and Wang, (1910) 1956).

Crompton, Louis, *Shaw the Dramatist* (Lincoln: University of Nebraska Press, 1969).

Dervin, Daniel, *Bernard Shaw: A Psychological Study* (Lewisburg, Pennsylvania: Bucknell University Press, 1975).

Dukore, Bernard, *Bernard Shaw, Director* (Seattle: University of Washington Press, 1971).

Irvine, William, *The Universe of G. B. S.* (New York: McGraw-Hill, 1949).

Kaye, Julian, *Bernard Shaw and the Nineteenth-Century Tradition* (Norman: University of Oklahoma Press, 1958).

Meisel, Martin, *Shaw and the Nineteenth-Century Theatre* (Princeton: Princeton University Press, 1963).

Morgan, Margery M., *The Shavian Playground: An Exploration of the Art of George Bernard Shaw* (London: Methuen, 1972).

Ohmann, Richard, *Shaw: The Style and the Man* (Middletown, Connecticut: Wesleyan University Press, 1962).

Turco, Alfred, *Shaw's Moral Vision: The Self and Salvation* (Ithaca, New York: Cornell University Press, 1976).

Valency, Maurice, *The Cart and the Trumpet* (New York: Oxford University Press, 1973).

Watson, Barbara Bellow, *A Shavian Guide to the Intelligent Woman* (New York: Norton, 1972).

Wisenthal, J. L., *The Marriage of Contraries: Bernard Shaw's Middle Plays* (Cambridge, Massachusetts: Harvard University Press, 1974).

4. Criticism: Periodicals and Collections

The periodical literature on Shaw is vast. Useful starting points are the collections listed below and the journals devoted exclusively to Shaw: *The Shavian* (London) and *The Independent Shavian* (New York). *The Shaw Review* has now been superseded by *The Annual of Bernard Shaw Studies*, which continues *The Shaw Review*'s Checklist of Shaviana.

Holroyd, Michael (ed.), *The Genius of Shaw* (London: Hodder and Stoughton, 1979).

Kaufmann, R. J. (ed.), *G. B. Shaw: A Collection of Critical Essays* (Englewood Cliffs, New Jersey: Prentice-Hall, 1965).

Kronenberger, Louis (ed.), *George Bernard Shaw: A Critical Survey* (New York: World, 1953).

Index

Achurch, Janet 68, 104, 105

Admirable Bashville, The 134–5

Anderson, Robert 105

Androcles and the Lion 176

Antoine, André 76

Apple Cart, The 79, 204–6

Archer, William 16, 17, 18, 22, 81, 82

Arms and the Man 3, 24, 99–104, 199

Attlee, Clement 33

Augier, Émile 18

Back to Methuselah 45, 47, 49, 50, 52, 58, 60, 79, 117, 131, 190, 194–5, 202

Balfour, Arthur 26

Barrett, Wilson 176

Barrie, Sir James M. 105

Bentley, Eric 37, 185

Berenson, Bernard 107

Bergson, Henri 50

Bernhardt, Sarah 70

Besant, Annie 33

Blake, William 41

Browning, Robert 186

Bunyan, John 4

Buoyant Billions 211

Butler, Samuel 41–9, 160

Caesar and Cleopatra 4, 9, 20, 36, 42, 61–2, 76, 126–32, 133

Calvert, Louis 75

Campbell, Mrs Patrick 22, 68, 71, 104, 176, 177

223

Candida 12, 21, 24, 25, 35, 61, 67, 99, 104–15, 138, 145, 154, 170, 174
Captain Brassbound's Conversion 77, 78, 79, 132–3, 134
Carlyle, Thomas 28, 114–15, 151
Cashel Byron's Profession 134
Chekhov, Anton 2, 54, 56, 190
Comte, Auguste 49
Cornell, Katherine 196
Creative Evolution 5, 38–53, 55, 60, 120, 165, 190

Daly, Arnold 105, 154
Dark Lady of the Sonnets, The 58
Darwin, Charles 41–2
Dervin, Daniel 21
Devil's Disciple, The 21, 25, 73, 76, 120–6, 137, 176
Dickens, Charles 55, 171, 184
Doctor's Dilemma, The 75, 76, 90, 170–2
Don Juan in Hell 135, 136, 138, 139
Duse, Eleonora 70

Edward VII 26
Erikson, Erik 8, 20

Fabian Essays in Socialism 30, 34, 36
Fabian Society 16, 17, 22, 32–6, 38, 68, 179
Fanny's First Play 175
Farr, Florence 20, 23, 89
Forbes-Robertson, Sir Johnston 126, 176
Franco, Francisco 210
Freud, Sigmund 183, 189, 190, 201

Geneva 203, 209–10
George, Henry 15–16, 31
Getting Married 72, 173–4
Gilbert, Sir William S. 121, 204
Gladstone, William 35
Goethe, Johann Wolfgang von 4, 48, 49, 51, 58
Granville-Barker, Harley 25, 105, 135, 148, 170
Great Catherine 187
Grein, Jacob Thomas 23, 81, 91

Heartbreak House 135, 151, 187–94, 207
Hitler, Adolph 37, 209
Hoffman, E.T.A. 184
Horniman, Annie Elizabeth 24
How He Lied to Her Husband 154
Hyndman, Henry Mayers 16

Ibsen, Henrik 2, 22, 54,
  56, 64–8, 68–9, 71–2,
  105, 106
Immaturity 13
'*In Good King Charles's
  Golden Days*' 210
*Intelligent Woman's Guide
  to Socialism and
  Capitalism, The* 202
Irvine, William 35
Irving, Sir Henry 19, 68,
  74, 116

Jevons, W. Stanley 29,
  31
Joad, C.E.M. 43
*John Bull's Other
  Island* 25, 147–54
Jones, Henry Arthur 69,
  70

Lamarck, Pierre de Monet
  de 44–6, 48
Lawrence, T.E. ('of
  Arabia') 26, 206
Lee, George John
  Vandeleur 10, 12, 14
Lenihan, Winifred 196
Lenin, V.I. 208
Life Force 5, 28, 52, 107,
  117, 137, 139, 147, 153,
  154, 163, 173, 174, 175,
  180, 190, 191, 194, 199,
  208, 211
London Music 10, 11

McCarthy, Lillah 75

Major Barbara 2, 7, 9,
  32, 33, 62–4, 75, 76, 82,
  119, 135, 154–70, 181,
  187, 197
Malvern Festival 203,
  211
Man and Superman 1,
  49, 67, 78, 79, 85, 90,
  135–47, 148, 190, 194,
  197
Man of Destiny, The 24,
  99, 116–17, 154
Mansfield, Richard 24,
  25, 89, 104, 120
Marlowe, Christopher
  135
Marx, Karl 16, 29, 30
Mill, John Stuart 28,
  46
Millionairess, The 209
Misalliance 72, 173, 174,
  190, 198
Molière (Jean Baptiste
  Poquelin) 55, 171
Mommsen, Theodor 126
Morgan, Margery M. 107
Morris, William 34, 35
Mozart, Wolfgang
  Amadeus 18
*Mrs Warren's
  Profession* 23, 27, 38,
  73, 80, 91–9, 100, 102,
  155, 156, 197
Music Cure, The 187
Mussolini, Benito 208,
  209
My Fair Lady 181

Index

Napoleon
(Bonaparte) 208
Nelson, Raymond S. 112
Nietzsche, Friedrich 41,
51, 61, 117

Offenbach, Jacques 187,
204
Oliver, Sidney 33
On the Rocks 207–8, 209
Overruled 187

Pascal, Gabriel 76
Pater, Walter 2
Patterson, Jenny 19, 20,
89, 90, 147
Pease, E.R. 33
Perfect Wagnerite, The
59–61, 127
Philanderer, The 20, 23,
89–91, 105, 118
Pinero, Arthur Wing 69–
70
Playlets of the War 187
Plays Pleasant 99–119
Plays Unpleasant 80–98,
99
Pre-Raphaelitism 106–7
Pygmalion, 14, 73, 76,
82, 130, 135, 176–86,
199

*Quintessence of Ibsenism,
The* 22, 64–7, 116

Reinhardt, Max 76, 126
*Revolutionist's Handbook,
The* 39, 135, 147

Ricardo, David 29, 30
Ruskin, John 28
Russell, Bertrand 33

Saint Joan 79, 135, 195–
201, 202, 203
Sardou, Victorien 71, 73–
4, 116
Schiller, Friedrich
von 121
Schopenhauer, Arthur
48, 59
Shakespeare, William 19,
51, 54, 56–9, 135, 211
Shakes versus Shav 211–
12
Shaw, Chalotte (wife) 21
Shaw, George Carr
(father) 6, 7
Shaw, Lucinda Elizabeth
Gurley (mother) 6, 9,
15
Shaw, Lucy (sister) 12,
13
Shelley, Mary 185
Shelley, Percy Bysshe 41,
51
*Shewing-up of Blanco
Posnet, The* 175
*Simpleton of the
Unexpected Isles,
The* 208–9
Stalin, Joseph 37
Stanislavsky,
Konstantin 76
Strindberg, August 2
Suetonius, Gaius 126

Sullivan, Sir Arthur 204

Terriss, William 25, 120
Terry, Dame Ellen 21,
    57, 74, 77–8, 89, 112,
    115, 116, 125, 132, 133,
    176
Thorndike, Dame
    Sybil 196
*Three Plays for
    Puritans* 119–33
*Too True to be
    Good* 206–7
Tree, Sir Herbert
    Beerbohm 77

Unsocial Socialist, An 14

Valency, Maurice, 15
Vedrenne, J.E. 25, 26,
    148

Wagner, Richard 18, 54,
    56, 59–64, 112, 123, 127
Walkley, A.B. 1, 135
Wallas, Graham 33
Webb, Beatrice 33, 107
Webb, Sidney 15, 16, 28,
    33, 36, 99
Wells, H.G. 33
Why She Would Not 211
Wicksteed, Philip H. 29
Widowers' Houses 23,
    24, 79, 80–9, 90, 100,
    102, 136, 137, 155, 201
Wilde, Oscar 2, 69, 84,
    92, 199

Yeats, William Butler 148
You Never Can Tell 24,
    99, 117–19, 130, 133,
    136